Key Stage 2

English Revision Guide

Carol Matchett

Schofield&Sims

Welcome to this book

This book will help you revise for the national tests in English at the end of Key Stage 2.

Sample texts help you to identify the features of different text types.

Blue headings show you which topic is covered.

Find out about words in **bold** by turning to the Glossary.

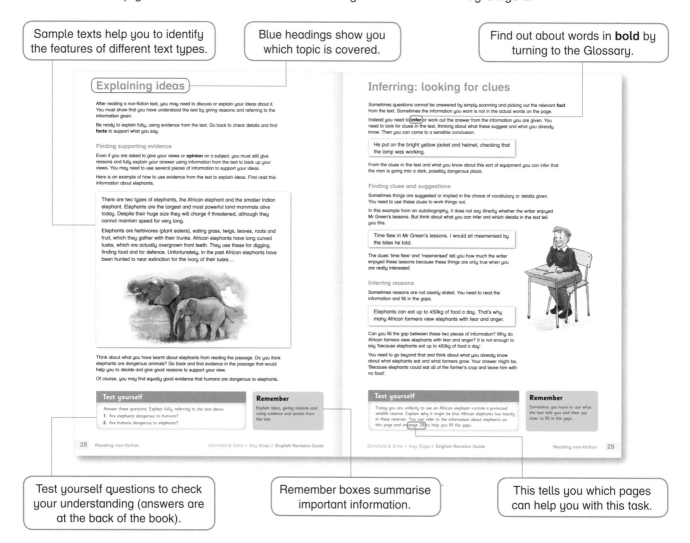

Test yourself questions to check your understanding (answers are at the back of the book).

Remember boxes summarise important information.

This tells you which pages can help you with this task.

How to revise

- Turn to the topic and read about it.
- Read the Remember box and then cover it up. Can you remember what it says?
- Read the Test yourself questions and write your answers on a piece of paper.
- Check your answers against the right answers at the back of the book.
- If you got any answers wrong, read the topic again, then have another go at the questions.
- If you got all the answers right – well done! Move on to the next topic.
- Once you have worked through this revision guide, move on to the **Key Stage 2 English Practice Papers**.

Tips for tests

- Always read the question carefully before you answer it.
- Have a go at as many of the questions as you can. If there is a question you really can't answer, just move on to the next one. You can always come back to it if you have time.
- Look out for questions that ask you to explain. This means that you must give reasons.
- If you have time at the end, check through your work.

Contents

Reading for meaning

When you are reading, it is important to think about what you read and to follow its meaning. Check that it makes sense. Think about what you already know on the topic, what you have just read and how the ideas link together.

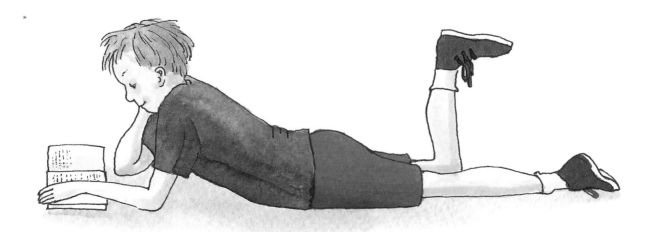

If you get confused or lose the meaning, stop. Think about what you have just read. Work out what you did not understand. Was it the meaning of a word? A confusing sentence? A complex idea? Then try these ideas to help you work out the meaning.

- Reread a confusing sentence – pay particular attention to the punctuation.
- Go back and reread the previous sentence in case the ideas link together.
- Go back and reread an earlier section to check a detail or some linked information.
- Make a note of a question to discuss or research later.
- Read on to see if the meaning becomes clearer.

Working out word meanings

It is important to work out the meaning of words when you are reading. Here are some techniques to help you.

- Read the complete sentence and work out the meaning of the word from the way it is used – think about another word or **synonym** that would make sense there.
- Remember that words can have different meanings in different contexts, for example:

  Do not disturb.   ⟵ *disturb (interrupt)*

  Some news stories disturb me.   ⟵ *disturb (upset/distress)*

- Check the meaning in a dictionary, or in the glossary if the book has one.
- Look for clues to word meaning in **root words**, **prefixes** and **suffixes** (see page 5).

Test yourself

What does the word in blue mean in each sentence?
1. He was absorbed in the book.
2. Tigers should not be kept in confined spaces.
3. It was an amazing spectacle.

Remember

Make sense of what you read. Use the rest of the sentence to work out the meaning of a word.

Root words, prefixes and suffixes

Root words

Many words are formed from root words with prefixes or suffixes added. Words with the same root belong to the same **word family** and have related meanings. Finding the root word can often give a clue to a word's meaning.

observant   observatory   observation

The examples above all come from the word 'observe', and are linked to the idea of 'watching carefully'.

Prefixes

Prefixes are added to the beginning of root words. They form new words by adding their own meaning to the root word.

interact (inter = between)	regroup (re = again)	substandard (sub = under/below)
antifreeze (anti = against)	prehistoric (pre = before)	superhuman (super = above/beyond)
misbehave (mis = wrongly)	automobile (auto = self)	overflow (over = too much)

Suffixes

Suffixes are added to the end of root words. They usually change words into a different **word class**.

observe is a **verb**   ⟶ I observe

adding –ant makes it into an **adjective** ⟶ I am observant

adding –ation makes it into a **noun**   ⟶ I make an observation

Here are some more examples of suffixes that change word classes.

pressurise	strengthen	originate	identify		⟵ forming verbs
tireless	respectful	agreeable	quarrelsome	historic	seasonal ⟵ forming adjectives
enjoyment	fitness	defender	formation	disturbance	stupidity ⟵ forming nouns

Putting together word meanings

You can use your knowledge of root words, prefixes and suffixes as well as the context to help you work out the meaning of words you meet when reading.

Moles live in an amazing subterranean world.   ⟵ sub (under) + terrain (land)

The interplanetary shuttle bus arrived.   ⟵ inter (between) + planet + ary

Test yourself

Write the meaning of the words in blue.
1. Purify the water.
2. He felt a bit overdressed.
3. The results were predictable.
4. She was full of admiration.
5. I was misinformed.
6. I can only sympathise.

Remember

Your knowledge of root words, prefixes, suffixes and word families can help you work out word meanings.

How to read a story

Reading a story seems straightforward – you start at the beginning and read to the end. However, real reading is much more than this. It involves thinking about the story, using your imagination and responding to what happens.

Try these techniques when you read a story.

- Think about the characters, the events and how you feel about them.
- Visualise or picture in your head the characters, the events and the settings, as they are described.
- **Predict** what might happen next from what you already know, or from hints and clues, then read on to find out if you are right.
- Make connections with your own experiences or with other stories you have read.

Asking questions

Ask yourself questions as you read the story. Here are some examples of the kinds of questions you might ask yourself to help you understand the story better.

- Why did that happen?
- Why did he or she do that?
- What would I have done?
- How do I feel about that? Why?
- How do I feel about this character?
- Is this like other stories I have read?

Making predictions

When you are making predictions, think about what you have already read, what has happened and what you know about the characters.

Look for hints and clues left by the author that suggest what is likely to happen, what a character might do or how the story could end. Use these details from the story to support your predictions.

When making predictions, use **phrases** like:

> I think/expect… because…
> …will probably… because…
> It says… which makes you think…
> We know… so I think…

Test yourself
Here is the first sentence of a story. What do you predict might happen?
Mum had told us a million times not to go into the cellar.

Remember

Think about the story. Look for clues that help you predict what might happen.

Following the main events

When you are reading a story, try to keep track of the main events – what happens, where and when. For example, you could remember what happens in each paragraph of a short story, or each chapter of a longer story or novel. This will help you remember the order in which events happen and how the events link together.

Knowing when important events happened is also useful if you want to go back later and check some details. You will be able to quickly find the part of the story that you need to look at.

At the start of the story

Identify the main characters, where or when the story is set, and what the story is about. Look out for an important event that will set off the chain of events that follows. For example:

In Treasure Island a mysterious pirate arrives at the Admiral Benbow inn. This event starts off an exciting adventure as the characters go searching for buried treasure.

As you read on

Identify and keep track of the main events as you read. You could try the following.

- Pause at the end of a page or chapter to think about what has happened and what you have learnt in that part of the story – why is a particular event important to the story?
- Identify problems, conflicts, complications and solutions – how do these move the story on?
- Mark important parts of the story so you can quickly go back and check details about the characters and events or find key sentences to refer to.
- Think of a suitable title for each chapter – something that summarises the chapter and reminds you of the main event.

At the end of the story

Think back over the whole story and try the following.

- Summarise the main events of the story in your own words.
- Select the five or six most important events in the story.
- List, note or draw the main events in the order they happened.
- Write a summary or **précis**, linking together the main events with words and phrases such as:

This story is about…	It starts when…	Then…
After that…	As a result…	But in the end…

- Go back and find key details about an important event.
- Retell the story or one important event from the story in your own words.

Test yourself

Remind yourself of the story 'Jack and the beanstalk'. Here are the main events in the story. Number them in the order they happened, then try retelling the story in your own words.

Jack climbs a beanstalk.

Jack steals a magic hen.

Jack exchanges his cow for beans.

Jack chops down the beanstalk.

Jack discovers a castle.

Remember

Identify and keep track of the main events in the story as you read.

Character details

Characters are vital to a story. As you read on, you learn more about the characters and you form ideas about them. You decide if a character is 'good' or 'bad', kind or mean, reliable or deceitful. Sometimes you might change your ideas about a character because of what happens later in the story.

Authors create characters through the details they give. This helps you to understand the characters and form ideas about them. When discussing a character, you need to refer to details in the text to explain your thoughts. These details might be in how characters are described, how they act or what they say (the dialogue).

Details by description

A description of a character's appearance might include some words or **phrases** that suggest what kind of person the character is.

A face appeared over the wall: a mop of sunny yellow hair, followed by two twinkling blue eyes, and a cheeky grin…

these details suggest that the character is friendly and fun

Details of actions

Actions can tell you a lot about a character.

Ellie would deliberately ignore the new girl. She would turn away with a flick of her hair and giggle loudly with her friends.

these details suggest that Ellie is unfriendly – she seems to be trying to make the new girl feel uncomfortable by leaving her out

Details in dialogue

Dialogue can give you clues about characters and the relationships between them. Look for details in how things are said as well as what is said.

'What are you doing here?' Max asked accusingly.
'I can come here if I like,' Ben replied, trying to sound calm.
'But what if I don't like,' Max said, giving Ben a cold stare.

these details suggest a tension between the two characters – Max is more powerful and aggressive

Ben is more wary

Test yourself

Mrs Pringle is kind and friendly. Find four details that support this idea.

Mrs Pringle was rather like a pillow – soft, comfortable and always there when needed. The children called her Granny Pringle, although she was actually no relation to them. But in times of trouble she was always there with her gentle words, cheery smile and delicious biscuits.

Remember

Look for details in description, actions and dialogue to support your ideas about the characters.

Character thoughts, feelings and motives

You need to think about characters' feelings, why they do things (their motives) and what they are thinking. Sometimes the author will tell you this information directly, but more often it is suggested in the character's actions and in how events are described. You need to **infer** or work out ideas from the information given.

As you read a story, look for clues about the characters' feelings and thoughts. Ask yourself why characters behave as they do. Remember, the clues are always in the story, so you must refer to the text when discussing feelings and motives.

Inferring thoughts and feelings

Rather than telling you directly how a character feels, authors often indicate feelings through actions and behaviour. You should look for clues that suggest a character's feelings.

> Joe slumped in a chair, his shoulders hunched. He defiantly pulled his cap down over his eyes and muttered to the empty room, 'Well, I don't care. I didn't want to go anyway.'

Joe's actions *suggest that he is feeling upset*

although he *says he doesn't care, his behaviour suggests that he does*

Inferring motives

You often have to work out a character's motives from what you are told. Look for details and clues that suggest why a character does or says something.

> Quickly Lucy opened the cupboard door and rummaged inside.

these words *suggest that Lucy is looking for something and is in a hurry*

Explaining inferences – referring to the text

When explaining a character's thoughts, feelings or motives, you need to refer to evidence from the text to explain your views. A character might have a mixture of thoughts and feelings at a key moment so you may need to mention a number of details.

> Breathing unsteadily, Nick sat on the very edge of his bed. He looked down at the envelope held between his trembling fingers. He turned it over. It was not properly sealed. It would be easy to open. He could quite easily read the contents and then put it back without anyone knowing.

these details *suggest that he is nervous*

these details *suggest that he is uncertain – tempted to do it... but not sure*

Test yourself

Read this passage. Explain fully what it shows about the character's thoughts and feelings at this moment. Use evidence from the text to support your ideas.

Although he walked as slowly as he could, he still came to the gate all too quickly. He looked around, hoping for something to distract him from lifting the catch and walking up the overgrown path. There was nothing. He felt a cold fist clench in his stomach...

Remember

Look for details and clues to help explain characters' thoughts, feelings and motives.

Different viewpoints

It is important to recognise viewpoint in stories because it affects your view of events and your impression of (or response to) the characters.

Some stories are written in the first **person**, from the viewpoint of one character. This means that you see events and the other characters through this person's eyes.

Often stories are written in the third person, as if the author is watching and describing the events. However, there is usually still one character you feel closest to – you see events from this character's viewpoint.

First person viewpoint

This extract is from a story told in the first person from the viewpoint of one of the characters. Look for clues that show the narrator's view of Rashid. Think about how Rashid sounds to you.

these details show the narrator's view of Rashid

clues that others may have a different view

To me Rashid always seemed different to the other lads. He joined in with the rest of us, joking around or playing football but somehow he was just different. He told these most amazing stories. The others would listen at first but then quickly tire of his talk and drift away. But not me – I found them enthralling and could listen for hours.

The narrator gives their view of Rashid, but there are clues that not everyone would agree. The overall effect is to make you want to know more about Rashid.

Third person viewpoint

In this example, the story is told in the third person, but you still see events from the viewpoint of one particular character. What impression do you get of Evie? How does she feel? How do you feel about her – and about the other characters?

Evie could hear laughing and giggling through the cloakroom door. Were they laughing at her? She was sure they were. She was always on the outside – always on the other side of the door.

this is what Evie thinks

From the clues in the text you might describe Evie as a loner or feeling left out. You might think that the other girls are being unkind on purpose. But things might appear very different from inside the cloakroom. You would have to look for clues in the rest of the story to find out which is true.

Test yourself

Read this extract from 'Cinderella – a sister's story'. How does it create a different impression of Cinderella and her sisters? Refer to the text to explain your answer.

Cinderella! You don't know her like I do. She goes around telling all sorts of lies about my sister and me. Just because she is so pretty, she gets away with everything.

Remember

The viewpoint used in a story will affect your view of the events and the characters.

Story structure

Authors shape or **structure** their stories to make them effective and to keep you reading. They may build the story around a mystery or intriguing puzzle to be solved. Or they may order the events to hide some information or create a surprise.

A story is usually built up with moments of tension and excitement leading to a satisfying ending. As you read, notice how the story builds up. Look for changes in mood and pace.

When you find a really effective part, ask yourself: How did the writer make that work? Think about how the episode is built up and how language and sentence features are used to help make it effective.

Building tension

Here is a paragraph that builds tension and creates suspense. Read it aloud in your head so you can hear the sound of the text. Notice how it is structured to build up the tension, and how the language and sentence features help create this effect.

using questions to make you wonder

repeating a pattern to build up tension – getting closer...

Stepping onto the landing, he closed the door behind him. He stood in the sudden darkness, listening.

How would he find his way without a light? What if someone heard him? His heart began to beat faster.

He took a long, slow breath. And another. Slowly, he felt his way past the first door, where his brother was sleeping; past the second door, where he could hear his father snoring. Now he felt the handle of the third door. It clicked open...

describing atmosphere

showing feelings

delaying and slowing events down

Creating action and excitement

Notice how the mood changes in different parts of a story. For example, sudden bursts of excitement and action like this:

exclamation mark

short sentence fragments for impact and pace

The wolves were close behind! Scrambling **madly** through the trees, the branches catching in her hair, she fought on. Struggling. Stumbling. Desperate. Not daring to look round, knowing they were behind her. Hearing their howls. Feeling the thud of their paws.

***verbs** suggesting panic*

vivid description

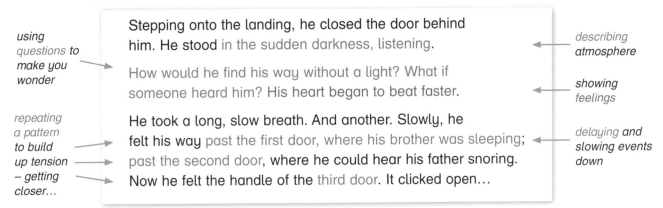

Test yourself

Read this passage. How does the writer build up the sense of mystery about the box? Explain fully, referring to the text in your answer.

On the dressing table, half-hidden behind a vase of wilting roses, was a small box. It was just a simple wooden box, but something about it seemed to draw him towards it. He moved the vase of flowers and stared at the box. He picked it up. It was surprisingly heavy. Perhaps there was something inside.

Remember

Think about how structure and language make the story effective.

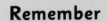

Language for effect

Words are the most important tool a writer has, so you know that the words used in a story have been carefully chosen for their meaning and for their effect (or impact) on the reader.

Words can suggest ideas, feelings and moods, as well as describe what things look or sound like.

Words for meaning and effect

When you are reading, think about words that you find particularly effective. Ask yourself why those words have been chosen.

Think about the impact of a word and what it suggests to you. What does it make you feel or think about? Remember that some words have more than one meaning – this might be why the writer has chosen them.

In this example, the word 'cold' is chosen for its meaning and impact. Think about the effect of this word in the sentence.

> She stepped out into the cold night air.

The word 'cold' tells you about the temperature outside, but it also sounds chilling and suggests something unpleasant or frightening might be waiting in the night. The effect is to make you feel worried about the person stepping outside.

Descriptions for effect

When you are reading descriptions, think about the effect of the words used. For example, think about the mood and impression created by the **noun phrases** in this extract.

these phrases suggest sadness and hardship →

The family sat around the simple wooden table.

A feeble light came from the small flickering fire,

casting gloomy shadows on the bare walls.

← *these phrases make you think the family is poor*

Verbs for impact

Verbs can have a powerful impact on the reader, and contribute further to feelings, mood and atmosphere.

People poured into the streets. Scrambling over each other in their haste to escape, jostling and pushing. Some struggling with belongings; others straining to keep their families together.

← *powerful verbs help create a sense of panic*

Test yourself

Read this sentence. Why has the word 'precious' been used to describe the prisoner's view of the sky through the window?

The prisoner lay on the stone floor in near darkness, staring up at the precious rectangle of blue sky, high above and out of reach.

Remember

Think about the effect of different words and what they make you think or feel.

Figurative language

Sometimes writers use **figurative language** such as **similes** and **metaphors** to create an effect. They are often chosen for their impact on the reader, perhaps making you think about the topic in a different way.

Similes and metaphors describe the subject by comparing it to something else. They help you to imagine and may suggest complex ideas or feelings about the subject.

Look out for examples of figurative language when you are reading. Think about what the image suggests to you and its impact on you. What does it make you think about? How does it make you feel or react? Think about why the writer has chosen to use that image.

Similes

A simile directly compares the subject with something else, using the words 'as' or 'like'.

She had a voice like velvet. ⟵ *this simile helps you imagine the voice – same qualities as velvet... smooth, soft, rich*

His face was as pale as the moonlight. ⟵ *this simile helps you picture his face, but also adds a sense of mystery*

The man moved like a panther stalking its prey. ⟵ *this simile tells you how the man moved (silently, stealthily, purposefully), but also makes you think that he is dangerous, like a panther hunting – sounds menacing and creates a sinister effect*

Metaphors

A metaphor compares the subject more indirectly (without using the words 'as' or 'like'). Metaphors can create powerful images for the reader that work on many levels.

The flames were tussling tigers pawing at the sky.

tussling tigers makes you think of fierceness and danger

tigers suggests the colour of the flames

pawing tigers creates an image of flames reaching up into the sky, again suggesting danger

Test yourself

Find the simile and metaphor used in this extract. Why did the writer choose these images?

The children spent every day of their holiday on the beach and the cave was a magnet for them. Inside the rocky chamber they felt like explorers on another planet.

Remember

Look out for similes and metaphors, and think about the effect they have.

Genre features and conventions

There are many different types, or genres, of stories (for example, fantasy, adventure, romance, horror). Each genre has its own special features such as typical characters, settings, events, themes and even language.

As you read a story, look out for familiar features that remind you of other stories you have read in the same genre.

Knowing the genre sometimes helps you to **predict** what will happen or how a story will end, as they often follow similar patterns. However, writers do not always follow these conventions – they may surprise you by introducing something completely different and unexpected.

Genre clues

Look for familiar features and conventions that tell you what type of story you are reading. For example, in this story opening you will find many features of a traditional tale.

typical opening – long ago   *typical characters – often stereotypes*

Long ago there lived a poor farmer. He lived with his wife in a little, stone farmhouse at the edge of the fields. One day the farmer was hard at work in his fields when an old man came by. The old man doffed his hat to the farmer and said: 'Good morning, young man. How would you like to be rich?'

Well, as you can imagine, the farmer was very surprised at this…

traditional setting – farm, fields

theme – rich and poor

language and style of the traditional storyteller

These features might lead you to expect certain events. But when you read the story, you will find out how the author has used these typical features, and whether there are any surprises.

Story titles

Even the title of a story can suggest the genre and lead you to expect a certain type of story.

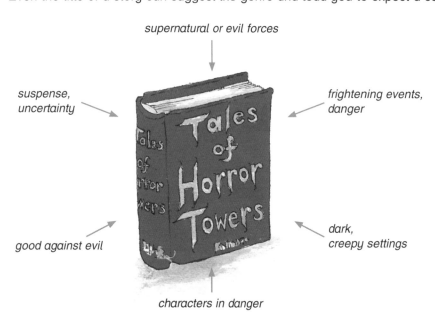

supernatural or evil forces

suspense, uncertainty

frightening events, danger

good against evil

dark, creepy settings

characters in danger

Remember

Look for familiar features in stories. Think about how the writer uses the expected conventions.

Test yourself

A book is described as science fiction. What features would you expect to find in this type of story?

Story themes

The theme of a story is the main idea that runs through it. Examples of story themes might be courage and heroism, the struggle between good and evil, dealing with a dilemma or overcoming a problem.

In some stories the theme is developed into a message for the reader. This is particularly true in traditional stories.

When you are thinking about story themes you need to take a step back and think about the whole story, everything that happens and the overall idea behind it. Sometimes themes and messages are clearly stated by the author, but more often they are suggested through the events and characters in the story.

Clues in the title

Titles can be useful in identifying themes as they give a clue to what the story is about. Here is an example of an anthology (or collection) of short stories.

this title suggests that all the stories will be about families, but the question mark hints that they might also be about problems that can occur within families…

Clearly stated themes

Here is an example where the theme of the story is clearly introduced in the opening sentence. The story begins:

> Secrets can be dangerous things…

This theme is developed in the rest of the story: someone has a secret and it causes problems.

Messages for the reader

Authors sometimes use the events in a story to convey a message, either leaving the reader to **infer** it, or stating it clearly. For example, in a fable such as 'The hare and the tortoise', the events illustrate a moral given at the end of the story.

> Slow and steady wins the race.

Test yourself

What is the theme of this story? Explain your answer referring to the events.

Two hungry brothers find a chapati lying on a stone. They argue about who found it and who should eat it. Neither will give in. In the end a stranger solves the problem. He eats it himself.

Remember

When looking for themes, think about the whole story, its events and characters.

Recommending stories

You may be asked to give your **opinion** about a book you have read or to recommend a story to others. When giving your opinion, there is no right and wrong answer. However, you should give reasons and explain why you like or recommend a story.

First think about what you liked about the story. Was it exciting, moving, sinister, humorous, interesting, entertaining, surprising, engrossing…? Then ask yourself the important question: Why? Which aspects of the story made it effective or a good read?

Explain your ideas by giving reasons, referring to key features and parts of the story.

Giving reasons

To explain why you liked a book, refer to different parts of the story, or to different aspects of the writing such as the plot, story **structure**, style or language.

starts by stating an opinion, describing the type of story

This is a thrilling adventure story about Abby, a lonely child who gets caught up in a robbery. It was really exciting, especially the part when Abby is trapped in the hideout. The author is really good at building up suspense and keeping you guessing. The ending is a real surprise. Help comes from someone very unexpected.

says what it is about

gives an example and explains why it is exciting, referring to the techniques used

comments on the plot and use of surprise

Supporting your opinions

Support your comments, using **phrases** like these to give reasons and refer to examples.

> It is full of…, for example,…
> There is a great part when…
> It is really…; for example, when…
> I particularly like how the author… because…

Making a recommendation

Not everyone likes the same sort of stories. You probably have your own reading preferences. So when recommending a story explain who would like it and why. You might compare it to other stories in the same genre or by the same author.

> Anyone who likes reading… stories will like this because…
> If you liked… then you might like this, because…

Test yourself

Think about a story that you have enjoyed reading recently and that you would recommend to others. Explain your choice by referring to different aspects of the story, and say who would enjoy it.

Remember

Explain your reasons for recommending a book, referring to the story and giving examples.

Making comparisons in fiction

When making comparisons you are thinking about how things are the same or different. You might be comparing two different stories, or comparing events or characters within a story.

Comparing within a story

Within a story you might compare:
- two characters:

  details about their appearance, qualities, actions or reactions to events
- the same character at the start and end of the story or before and after an event:

  evidence of how the character has changed as a result of experiences or events
- two events:

  what happens, why and the results of each
- two settings:

  different details, mood, atmosphere or events in each setting.

Comparing between stories

You might compare two stories (for example, two stories on the same theme, or by the same author, or two versions of the same story).

You might compare just one aspect of the two stories (for example, how the hero in each story is presented) or you could use a comparison grid like this to help you compare a number of aspects.

	Story 1	Story 2
Characters		
Settings		
Plot and story structure		
Themes		
Style		
Viewpoint		

Writing comparisons

When you are making comparisons you could use phrases like this.

A is... but B is...
Both A and B are...
A is described as... while B is described as...
It says A is... whereas B is said to be...

Test yourself

Think of a story you have read recently that has two very different characters. Explain two or three ways in which they are different, using comparison language like the phrases shown above.

Remember

When comparing stories, look for details that show or suggest how things are the same or different.

How to read a poem

Poems can be quite short, but they often have a lot to say. You can read a poem many times and each time notice something new and interesting that will help you understand it more.

When you first read a poem, read it aloud in your head so you can hear the sound of the words. What do you feel, see, think? Try to get the mood of the poem and a general idea of what it is about.

Then read the poem again. Read each verse carefully, checking it makes sense. Think about the main idea in each verse.

Here is a poem called 'The Sands of Dee' by Charles Kingsley. Try reading the poem aloud in your head. Then read the poem again and use the prompts to help you think about it.

The Sands of Dee

'O Mary, go and call the cattle home,
And call the cattle home,
And call the cattle home,
Across the sands of Dee';
The western wind was wild and dank with foam,
And all alone went she.

The western tide crept up along the sand,
And o'er and o'er the sand,
And round and round the sand,
As far as the eye could see.
The rolling mist came down and hid the land:
And never home came she.

'O is it weed, or fish, or floating hair –
A tress of golden hair,
A drownèd maiden's hair,
Above the nets at sea?'
Was never salmon yet that shone so fair
Among the stakes of Dee.

They rowed her in across the rolling foam,
The cruel crawling foam,
The cruel hungry foam,
To her grave beside the sea:
But still the boatmen hear her call the cattle home
Across the sands of Dee.

by Charles Kingsley

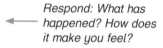
Visualise: Picture the events and scene.

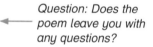
Respond: What has happened? How does it make you feel?

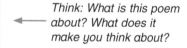
Question: Does the poem leave you with any questions?

Think: What is this poem about? What does it make you think about?

Test yourself

Write a one-line summary of the main event in each verse of this poem. Verse 1 has been done for you.

Verse 1: a girl goes to call the cattle home.

Remember

Read the poem aloud in your head. Think about the mood, images and main idea.

Reading closely

Each time you read a poem you will notice more details. Start to think about the meaning of individual words, **phrases** or lines and how they add to the poem. All these details help paint a picture and develop the main idea or theme of the poem.

Inferring meaning

Often in poems things are not clearly stated. The reader is left to **infer** or work things out from what is said or suggested. You need to look for clues in the text and bring in your own ideas to understand the meaning.

When you explain your thoughts, feelings and ideas about a poem, it is important to refer to the details in particular lines, words or phrases to support what you say.

In 'The Sands of Dee', the reader is not told directly what happened to the girl in the poem. You have to infer the full story from the details given.

For example:

- Mary goes alone to call the cattle home
- the tide comes in
- Mary never came home.

Based on this you can infer that Mary was drowned.

Test yourself

Reread the poem 'The Sands of Dee'. This time notice details about the events and how they are described. Use the prompts in these questions to help you refer to particular lines, words or phrases.

Verse 1: Which lines suggest that something bad is going to happen and make you worry about the girl?

Verse 2: Which details show the tide came in slowly?

Verse 3: Which lines tell you where the girl was found?

Verse 4: Which lines remind you that the sea is responsible for the girl's death?

Remember

Look for details and clues in a poem. Refer to lines or phrases to support your ideas about a poem.

Poetic language for effect

Poets choose words very carefully. Every word in a poem adds to the overall meaning and effect. Look out for words and **phrases** that you find particularly effective. Think about why the poet chose those words. How does their choice make you feel or react? What does it make you think about?

Remember that the choice of words is always linked to the ideas the poet is trying to put across. Think about the meaning of the word or phrase in that particular line, verse or poem and the effect it creates. A word might describe a sight, sound or feeling, or create a mood – or it might be used by the poet to suggest many of these things at once.

Expressive adjectives

Adjectives describe how things look, sound or feel but they can also suggest feelings and mood. For example, in the poem 'The Sands of Dee':

The western wind was wild and dank with foam,

the adjectives 'wild' and 'dank' describe the scene (blustery, damp, cold) and help create a dark and threatening mood

*the **alliteration** in 'the western wind was wild' further contributes to the mood – the repeated 'w' sounds wild and windy*

Powerful verbs

Verbs describe movements but they can also create feelings, moods and powerful effects. Here is an extract from the poem 'The Cataract of Lodore' by Robert Southey (a cataract is a waterfall). Think about what the verbs suggest about the water.

verbs chosen to suggest sudden, fast, wild movements

The cataract strong then plunges along;
Striking and raging as if a war waging
Its caverns and rocks among;

Rising and leaping, sinking and creeping,
Swelling and sweeping, showering and springing.
Flying and flinging, writhing and wringing ...

listing verbs to suggest the rushing speed of the water, ever moving without stopping

---

Test yourself

1. In the last verse of the poem 'The Sands of Dee' on page 18, find the adjectives used to describe the foaming sea.
2. Why do you think the poet chose these words?

Remember

Think about what a word or phrase suggests to you as it is used in the poem.

Figurative language

Poets often use imagery and **figurative language** to create pictures, express moods and suggest ideas.

For example, they might use:

- a **simile** or **metaphor** – comparing the thing they are describing to something else
- **personification** – describing a thing or idea as if it were a human being
- **alliteration** or **onomatopoeia** – creating effects through sound patterns.

Look out for examples of similes and metaphors in poems you read. Think about why the poet chose to make the comparison. What feature or quality does it suggest? What does it make you think about? Notice the effect. How does it make you feel? Remember figurative language is a powerful tool – it can suggest a number of different ideas.

Similes

A simile compares the subject to something else (using the word 'as' or 'like' – see page 13). The simile in this example is from 'The Cataract of Lodore' on page 20. What does it suggest about the water?

> The cataract strong then plunges along;
> Striking and raging as if a war waging

suggests the sound and fury of the water – the noise, battling, chaos, power and violence

Metaphors

Here is a metaphor from a poem about a winter morning. Think about the image and mood created.

> The snow was a carpet of whiteness,
> Rolled out across the fields.

describes the scene and creates a peaceful mood

Personification

Here is an example of personification taken from a poem describing a storm. Think about the effect and why the poet chose this dramatic image.

> Then lightning slashed the sky with an angry scar

makes lightning sound violent, dangerous

Test yourself

In the poem 'The Eagle', the poet (Alfred, Lord Tennyson) describes an eagle sitting on a cliff looking down at the sea. He ends with the lines:

> *He watches from his mountain walls,*
> *And like a thunderbolt he falls.*

Why do you think the poet compares the eagle to a thunderbolt?

Remember

When you read a simile or metaphor, think about the effect it creates and why the poet chose it.

Reciting and reading aloud

Poetry has a special sound. Many poems have a strong rhythm and rhyme. That is why they sound effective read aloud. Some use patterned language, which makes them easier to learn off by heart and recite.

When reciting a poem, or reading it aloud, always think about its meaning. Make the meaning clear as well as keeping the rhythm and rhyme.

Listening for rhythm and rhyme

Poems with a strong rhythm and rhyme are good for reading aloud. Here are some lines from a poem called 'From a railway carriage', by Robert Louis Stevenson. Read them aloud. Listen for the strong rhythm and rhyme. Think about the effect created.

> Faster than fairies, faster than witches,
> Bridges and houses, hedges and ditches;
> And charging along like troops in a battle,
> All through the meadows the horses and cattle:

the rhythm rattles along like the noise of the train hurrying along the track

Reciting short poems

The easiest poems to learn off by heart are short poems with a clear pattern and a strong rhythm and rhyme. For example, a limerick is only five lines long and has a very strict rhythm and rhyme. Try learning this limerick off by heart.

> There once was a dog known as Fred,
> Who wouldn't get out of his bed.
> He said: 'There's no way!
> I'll stay here all day –
> Until I desire to be fed.'

follow the punctuation to help make the meaning clear – it also helps to stress the rhyming words

Learning and reciting longer poems

When learning a longer poem, try to learn it a verse at a time. Sometimes it helps to picture each verse. Repeated lines, rhyme and patterned language will also help you learn the poem.

Always think about the meaning as you recite the poem. Think about how you can use your voice to show the mood and feelings of the poem.

Test yourself

Look again at the poem 'The Sands of Dee' on page 18. Think about how you could use your voice to recite it effectively. What features of the poem would help you remember it?

Remember

When reciting a poem, think about the meaning as well as keeping the rhythm and the rhyme.

Structure, form and presentation

Most poems have a shape and **structure**. They are made up of lines and often verses. The poet orders the lines and verses so that the poem builds up ideas or develops the theme. As you read a poem, think about how these ideas are built up.

There are also many different forms of poetry. Some of these have a very strict structure, such as a fixed number of lines, or **syllables** in a line. Others allow the poet more choice and freedom.

Learn to recognise the features of different forms and think about why the poet has chosen or used a particular form. For example, some poem forms are usually used for humorous poems, while others are usually descriptive.

Syllable structures

A haiku poem has a very strict structure. It is three lines long and each line must have the correct number of syllables – 5, 7, 5. Haiku poems are usually descriptive and focus on a single image or detail.

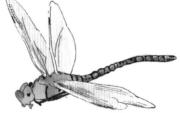

> Water, calm and still;
> Dragonflies hovering, not
> Touching the surface.

Poems with patterns

Some poems have a repeated pattern. There might be a repeated chorus or every verse or line might begin in the same way. Here is a poem made up of a list of kennings or short **phrases**, describing a subject that is not named. Can you guess what it is?

> Heat generator
> Sweat maker
> Skin burner
> Water stealer

Free verse

Free verse is poetry that has no clear form or structure. It sounds more like normal speech.

> The sun silent in the sky
>   watches as it warms
>   but says nothing.

Shape on the page

Sometimes the shape of the poem on the page, or how it is presented, reflects the subject of the poem. In shape poems, the words are formed or set out in the shape of the subject. In other poems, the poet might use a special style of lettering for parts of the poem or set out the lines to make a pattern.

Test yourself

Here is a line from a poem: *A frozen rime on sills and trees*

What is interesting about the letters in blue?

Remember

Think about the way form, structure and presentation add to a poem's meaning.

How to read non-fiction

Sometimes you read non-fiction texts to find a particular piece of information. On other occasions, you might read the whole text and think about the information it gives. How you read a non-fiction text depends on why you are reading it.

Before you begin reading, it is usually a good idea to skim through to get an idea of what it is about. You can see what aspects of the topic are covered or what type of text it is and how it is organised.

You can start to think about what you already know about the topic and about similar texts you have read. You can **predict** what the text might tell you and think of questions that you hope it will answer.

Skimming through the text will also help you to find particular pieces of information if you need to.

Using titles and headings

Titles and headings tell you what a text is about. They may also give clues about the type of text or its purpose. Ask yourself these questions.

- What am I reading?
- Why am I reading it?
- What do I know about this topic?
- What do I want to find out?

Getting an overview

Skim through the text looking at headings, sub-headings and illustrations. Get an idea of the content and how the text is organised. Start to make predictions about the writer's purpose and what the text will tell you.

For example, here are the headings from a book about cars, and some questions you could ask yourself.

> ### Horseless carriages: the first motorcars

> ### The start of mass production

> ### The golden age of motoring

> ### Designs today: speed, comfort and convenience

> ### The future of motoring

- How is it organised?
- What will it tell me?
- What won't it tell me?
- How will I read it and find the information I want?

Test yourself

Answer the four questions in the section 'Getting an overview' about the book on cars.

Remember

Skim through the text to get an overview before you read it. Start to predict and ask questions.

Text types, forms and features

The term non-fiction covers a whole range of books and texts. Textbooks, information books, reference books such as dictionaries and encyclopedias, magazines, leaflets, newspapers, letters and texts you read on screen are all non-fiction texts.

Features and purpose

Non-fiction texts are written for different purposes – such as to instruct, inform, recount, explain or persuade. We also read these texts for different purposes and in different ways. They have different features, which are designed to support the purpose and help you read them. For example, a recipe usually has a series of numbered steps because this makes it easy to follow.

Here are some examples of non-fiction text types and forms. Think of examples you have read and try to remember the features they use.

	Purpose	Examples	Features
Information texts	to give information on a topic	information book, leaflet, encyclopedia entry, magazine article, guidebook	grouped information, headings, sub-headings, pictures
Instructions	to tell how to do or achieve something	how to... book, cookbook, manual, recipe, rules, instruction leaflet	stated goal, series of numbered steps, list of equipment, sub-headings
Factual accounts	to recount events, say what happened	historical accounts, news or sports reports, diaries, biographies and autobiographies, eye-witness accounts	time or chronological order, third or first **person**, names, dates
Persuasive texts	to convince the reader/listener	posters, adverts, fliers and leaflets, letters to newspapers, speeches	**opinions**, persuasive language, rhetorical questions, appealing ideas and/or pictures

Mixed texts

A non-fiction text will often contain a mixture of different text types, such as:

- a magazine – might include reports, interviews, instructions, letters
- a newspaper article – might explain an issue and discuss different views on it
- a recipe – might include tempting descriptions and nutritional information as well as instructions.

Test yourself

In what type of text would you expect to find these sentences?
1. Brachiosaurus, a plant-eater, was the largest land animal ever known.
2. Next, add the oats and mix well together.
3. I left school at sixteen...

Remember

Look for features used in a particular type of text or form of writing.

Summarising the main ideas

When you read non-fiction, it is important to think about the ideas and information given. Stop at the end of a piece of text or at the end of a section and think about the main ideas and important or useful details.

Finding and noting ideas

You could try these techniques to help identify and summarise the main ideas as you read.

- Keep a note of the main idea in each section.
- Use text marking to note key details that support the main idea (for example, underlining key words or **phrases**).
- Decide which parts are helpful or relevant to what you want to find out, if you have a particular task.
- Summarise what you have learnt in your own words when you have finished reading.
- Write a **précis** or written summary including the main ideas.

Here is some information about the solar system. Read it through, stopping to identify the main idea and thinking which key details you would note.

The solar system

The solar system is made up of the Sun, the planets that orbit the Sun and other bodies such as moons, comets and meteorites.

The inner planets, those closest to the Sun, are Mercury, Venus, Earth and Mars. These planets are small and rocky with a solid surface. Beyond a belt of asteroids lie the outer planets: Jupiter, Saturn, Uranus and Neptune. These are huge giants made from gases and liquids. They have no solid surface.

Mercury, the closest planet to the Sun, is also the smallest. It orbits the Sun once every 88 days. Like many of the inner planets it has no moons. Jupiter, the fifth planet from the Sun, is the largest in the solar system. It takes twelve Earth years to orbit the Sun and like the other outer planets it has dozens of moons.

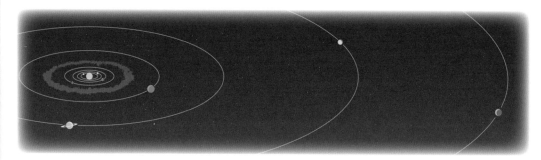

Test yourself

Think about the information given in the three paragraphs above.

1. Which of these would be the most suitable replacement heading? 'The inner and outer planets' or 'A planet's moons'?
2. Write down four or five key differences between the inner and outer planets.

Remember

Identify and summarise the main ideas as you read through a non-fiction text.

Finding and recording information

Sometimes you need to find a piece of information or gather together various pieces of information to complete a task. Make sure you are clear about what information you need. Identify key words and then scan the text looking for these words to help you find the information quickly.

All the information may not be in one place. Keep scanning and reading to find all the information needed.

Gathering and presenting information

A note-making or summary table is a useful way of gathering and recording information. Here is an example that could be used to gather information about planets in the solar system.

	Mercury	Earth	Jupiter
Position		3rd from the Sun	
Description		small and rocky	
Orbit		365 ¼ days	
Moons		one	

planet names are the key words to scan for in the text

down the side is a list of information to find

Comparing information

A note-making table can also help you to compare information you find in a text. For example, here you might want to compare information about two of the planets. You can record **facts** about each planet and then look for similarities and differences.

Test yourself

1. Use the information from page 26 to find the missing details in the table, about Mercury and Jupiter.
2. Find one difference between Earth and Mercury.

Remember

Scan the text for key words to help you find the information you are looking for.

Explaining ideas

After reading a non-fiction text, you may need to discuss or explain your ideas about it. You must show that you have understood the text by giving reasons and referring to the information given.

Be ready to explain fully, using evidence from the text. Go back to check details and find **facts** to support what you say.

Finding supporting evidence

Even if you are asked to give your views or **opinion** on a subject, you must still give reasons and fully explain your answer using information from the text to back up your views. You may need to use several pieces of information to support your ideas.

Here is an example of how to use evidence from the text to explain ideas. First read this information about elephants.

There are two types of elephants, the African elephant and the smaller Indian elephant. Elephants are the largest and most powerful land mammals alive today. Despite their huge size they will charge if threatened, although they cannot maintain speed for very long.

Elephants are herbivores (plant eaters), eating grass, twigs, leaves, roots and fruit, which they gather with their trunks. African elephants have long curved tusks, which are actually overgrown front teeth. They use these for digging, finding food and for defence. Unfortunately, in the past African elephants have been hunted to near extinction for the ivory of their tusks...

Think about what you have learnt about elephants from reading the passage. Do you think elephants are dangerous animals? Go back and find evidence in the passage that would help you to decide and give good reasons to support your view.

Of course, you may find equally good evidence that humans are dangerous to elephants.

Test yourself

Answer these questions. Explain fully, referring to the text above.

1. Are elephants dangerous to humans?
2. Are humans dangerous to elephants?

Remember

Explain ideas, giving reasons and using evidence and details from the text.

Inferring: looking for clues

Sometimes questions cannot be answered by simply scanning and picking out the relevant fact from the text. Sometimes the information you want is not in the actual words on the page.

Instead you need to **infer** or work out the answer from the information you are given. You need to look for clues in the text, thinking about what these suggest and what you already know. Then you can come to a sensible conclusion.

> He put on the bright yellow jacket and helmet, checking that the lamp was working.

From the clues in the text and what you know about this sort of equipment you can infer that the man is going into a dark, possibly dangerous place.

Finding clues and suggestions

Sometimes things are suggested or implied in the choice of vocabulary or details given. You need to use these clues to work things out.

In this example from an autobiography, it does not say directly whether the writer enjoyed Mr Green's lessons. But think about what you can infer and which details in the text tell you this.

> Time flew in Mr Green's lessons. I would sit mesmerised by the tales he told.

The clues 'time flew' and 'mesmerised' tell you how much the writer enjoyed these lessons because these things are only true when you are really interested.

Inferring reasons

Sometimes reasons are not clearly stated. You need to read the information and fill in the gaps.

> Elephants can eat up to 450kg of food a day. That's why many African farmers view elephants with fear and anger.

Can you fill the gap between these two pieces of information? Why do African farmers view elephants with fear and anger? It is not enough to say 'because elephants eat up to 450kg of food a day'.

You need to go beyond that and think about what you already know about what elephants eat and what farmers grow. Your answer might be, 'Because elephants could eat all of the farmer's crop and leave him with no food'.

Test yourself

Today you are unlikely to see an African elephant outside a protected wildlife reserve. Explain why it might be that African elephants live mainly in these reserves. You can refer to the information about elephants on this page and on page 28 to help you fill the gaps.

Remember

Sometimes you have to use what the text tells you and then use clues to fill in the gaps.

Fact and opinion

You might think that everything you read in a non-fiction book is pure **fact** – that it is definitely true. But this is not always the case.

Writers often include their **opinions** as well as factual information. An opinion is what some people believe. It is not definitely true and cannot be proved. Some people may have different views or opinions on the subject.

Recognising fact and opinion

It is important to recognise facts and opinions when you are reading. Many non-fiction texts include a mixture of both. For example, a sports report gives facts about the event or game but it may also include some of the writer's opinions. A persuasive letter will give the writer's opinions but these will probably be backed up by facts.

Here is some information about a ruined building. Look out for an opinion slipped in with the facts.

> The ruins of Mately Hall stand on the banks of the river. Originally built in the 1570s, during the reign of Elizabeth I, it was the home of the Mately family for 350 years. After a fire in 1922 the family could not afford to restore the building and it has been left as a ruin ever since. Really the local council should save the building, not leave it unprotected…

most of the information is fact, but this is an opinion – the writer believes it but others may disagree

Opinions that look like facts

Sometimes a writer's opinion shows up in how they present the facts. Here is an extract from a newspaper report on a football match. Look out for a word showing the writer's opinion.

> Rovers were unlucky to lose their lead just before half time when Robinson shot low past the goalkeeper.

it is a fact that Rovers lost their lead and Robinson scored, but an opinion that it was unlucky

Test yourself

Read this paragraph. Find the sentence that gives the opinion of the writer rather than being a definite fact.

The author Tamsin Black wrote her first novel in 1992. Since then she has written over 20 books. She is the best current writer of realistic stories. Her most recent novel will be published next month.

Remember

A fact is definitely true and can be proved. An opinion is just the view of some people.

Different viewpoints

When researching a topic, you might read different texts on the same topic to compare the information given. Different writers might have different purposes or different views on the subject. This might influence what information they give or how they present it.

Look out for opinions or signs of the writer's viewpoint when you are reading.

Inferring the writer's view

Writers sometimes state their views quite clearly. For example:

> To me this was a ridiculously dangerous decision.

> It seems obvious that electric cars are the way forward.

But often you have to **infer** the writer's views from clues in the text. In this example, think about the choice of words in these two statements and what they suggest about the writer's thoughts on the subject.

> This magnificent ruin stands on the banks of the river.   ← shows the writer's *positive* view of the ruin
> Some idiot had painted graffiti on the walls.   ← shows the writer's *negative* view of the graffiti

The writer probably wants to persuade readers to think the same.

Texts with different views

In some non-fiction texts, writers choose to present the reader with different views on a subject. They do this by presenting facts and explaining the different views. They also use quotations.

Quotations clearly show the view of a particular named person. For example, in an article on a historic building the writer includes this quotation:

> Professor Ballinger of the Buildings Protection League claims: ←   *quotation tells you what one expert claims or argues*
> 'This building is very important. It helps us to understand the history of the local area.'

The writer may balance this by including another quotation from someone with a different viewpoint. For example:

> On the other hand, Mrs Hunter of the Mately District Council argues: 'Why worry about the history of the area? The future is more important.'

The writer leaves it for the reader to decide who is right, by considering the information and arguments given in the article.

Test yourself

This sentence appears in an article on spiders:

> *These captivating creatures deserve our respect and should be admired.*

What does the writer think about spiders? How can you tell?

Remember

Look out for clues that show the writer's viewpoint and purpose.

Structure and presentation

Non-fiction texts are organised and presented differently from stories. Stories usually have a time or chronological **structure** but non-fiction texts are often structured in different ways (for example, by topic).

Features such as sub-headings or numbering show how the information is organised and help the reader know how to read the text.

Presentation features

You will notice that other presentation features such as text boxes, bold print, bullet points, tables of information and diagrams are often used in non-fiction texts. These features help present information clearly. They draw attention to important information and make it easier for the reader to follow, or to find the information needed.

Look out for these presentation features. Think about why the writer has chosen to use them and how they help you to read the text effectively.

Here is an example of an article about bird watching. Look at how the information has been presented and think about the purpose of each feature.

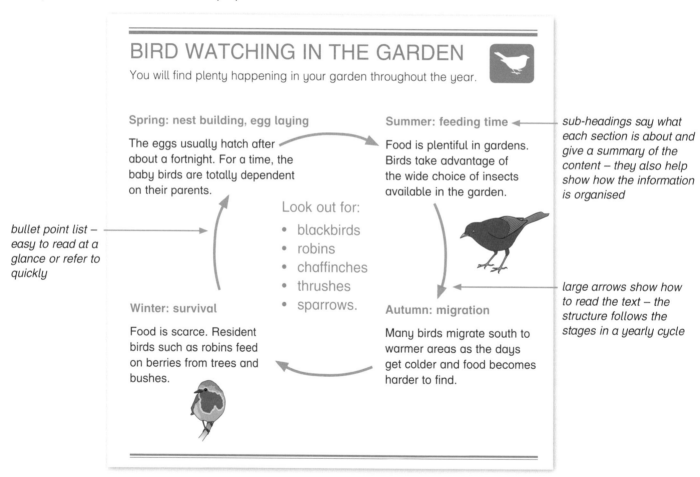

BIRD WATCHING IN THE GARDEN
You will find plenty happening in your garden throughout the year.

Spring: nest building, egg laying

The eggs usually hatch after about a fortnight. For a time, the baby birds are totally dependent on their parents.

Summer: feeding time

Food is plentiful in gardens. Birds take advantage of the wide choice of insects available in the garden.

Look out for:
- blackbirds
- robins
- chaffinches
- thrushes
- sparrows.

Winter: survival

Food is scarce. Resident birds such as robins feed on berries from trees and bushes.

Autumn: migration

Many birds migrate south to warmer areas as the days get colder and food becomes harder to find.

sub-headings say what each section is about and give a summary of the content – they also help show how the information is organised

bullet point list – easy to read at a glance or refer to quickly

large arrows show how to read the text – the structure follows the stages in a yearly cycle

Test yourself

In a set of instructions called 'How to make a kite', why do you think the following features are used?

1. a bullet point list for items needed

2. numbered steps

3. diagrams for some steps

Remember

Look at how information is structured and presented. Think about why it is organised and presented in this way.

Language for effect

Non-fiction writers use language to express ideas and information clearly. Often they use a lot of precise, technical words relating to the topic but they also use descriptive language to help you picture or imagine what they are writing about.

They also use language to create an effect, to capture our interest and to suggest ideas to the reader.

Notice words and **phrases** that stand out to you. Think about these words and their impact on you – what they make you think about, how they make you feel. This will help you understand why the writer chose them.

Capturing the reader's interest

Non-fiction writers use language to capture your interest and make the information sound exciting. For example, think about the effect of starting like this:

Imagine an endless expanse of sand stretching as far as you can see. ◀── *makes you think about the subject and captures your interest and imagination*

Or like this:

Killer crocodiles! ◀── *uses **alliteration** to grab your attention*

Choosing words for effect

Some words are chosen for their effect on the reader. Think about the effect of the words in this example – the ideas they suggest, the impression they create and what they make you think or feel.

The poor, trembling creatures trapped in cages far from home. ◀── *makes you feel sorry for the animals – 'trapped' sounds like they cannot escape, 'trembling' makes them seem scared*

Using figurative language

Similes and **metaphors** might be used to help you picture the subject, to suggest ideas or to create particular effects. For example, think about the impressions created by these images:

The trees in a rainforest form a vast rooftop garden. ◀── *suggests the colourful richness of the rainforest*

Simmons played with about as much grace as an injured rhinoceros. ◀── *mocks the clumsy quality of the footballer's play*

Test yourself

Read this information from a book on dinosaurs. Why does the writer describe T-Rex as like 'a mouth on legs'? Give two reasons.

The Tyrannosaurus Rex, a meat-eater, could open its mouth wide enough to eat 70kg of meat in just one bite. Always on the look-out for food, T-Rex was like a mouth on legs!

Remember

Think about the meaning and effect of words used by non-fiction writers.

Making comparisons in non-fiction

You might be asked to look at an information text and compare information (or identify what is the same and what is different) about two different people, places, items or events. Or you might read an account of an event or an explanation of a process and compare things at the beginning and end of the process.

To make comparisons you need to read carefully and find details about the two things you are comparing. Think about what is the same and what is different.

Comparing two texts

You might compare two texts on the same topic, perhaps comparing the information they give. Think about what is the same and what is different.

You might also think about the purpose and features of each text. Are they the same? How are they different? Ask yourself some questions.

- Did both writers have the same purpose – to inform, persuade, instruct…?
- Did they have the same audience in mind? Perhaps one text was aimed at adults and one at younger readers? How do you know?
- Did the writers have a particular view or angle on the subject?
- How were the texts **structured** and presented? Was one easier to use? Did one text use illustration, diagrams or photographs to give information?
- What were they like to read? How would you describe the style – was it **formal**, or chatty and friendly? What features helped to capture or keep your interest?

Explaining what you find

Once you have noted things that are the same and different you can write your comparison, explaining fully. Use **phrases** such as:

> Both A and B are…
>
> A is… but B is…
>
> It says A is…, which shows…, whereas B…

For example:

> Both texts are about endangered animals. The first text gives factual information, while the second text gives the writer's view on what should be done to save the animals. In the first text the information is presented in fact boxes and bullet points so it is easy to pick out key facts. In contrast, you have to read the second text from the start to the end. The second text makes you think more about the subject. For example, it begins: 'Imagine a world with no wild animals.'

compares a number of features

makes a comment supported by an example and quotation from the text

Test yourself

Think of two non-fiction texts you have read recently on the same subject. State two things that are different about the purpose or features used in these texts.

Remember

Read carefully, looking for aspects of the information that are the same or different.

Writing in sentences

When we write, we write in sentences. So whenever you are writing, it is a good idea to think in sentences. These sentences are made up of words, **phrases** and **clauses**. A phrase is a group of words that go together. For example:

the small fox   ⟵ *a **noun** phrase built around the word 'fox'*

A clause is a group of words that includes a **verb**. For example:

the small fox ran

Single-clause sentences

A sentence has at least one clause. A single-clause sentence has one main clause. Here are some examples of sentences with just one clause. In each sentence the **subject** (who or what the sentence is about) is followed by a verb.

The boy waited.

The ground shook.   *very short sentences like these stand out and can have a strong impact*

The forest was ablaze.

In this next example, the sentence has a subject, a verb and then an **object** (someone or something affected by the action).

The dog ate the cake.

Sentences with co-ordinating conjunctions

You can join two or more sentences or main clauses together using the co-ordinating **conjunctions** 'and', 'but', 'or'.

He was late. He missed the bus. ⟶ He was late and he missed the bus.

She shouted. No-one heard. ⟶ She shouted but no-one heard.

I could wait. I could go home. ⟶ I could wait or I could go home.

Test yourself

Complete these sentences.

1. He could have gone left or _____ but _____.
2. She opened the door and _____ but _____.
3. We could hurry and _____ or _____.

Remember

Use co-ordinating conjunctions to join two main clauses.

Sentence types

There are different types of sentence:

- statements
- questions
- commands
- exclamations.

Using different types of sentence helps to bring variety to your writing.

Statements

A statement is a sentence that tells you something. It usually has a **subject** followed by a **verb**. For example:

> The day was cold.
>
> Charles Dickens was born in 1812.

Questions

A question asks something and usually needs a response or an answer. Questions often start with question words, such as:

> Who was outside?   What do you think?   Where is it?   ⟵ *questions always end with a question mark*

Some questions are formed by reordering the words in a statement.

> Is there life on another planet?
>
> Could you drive a Grand Prix car?
>
> Would you like to try?

In **informal** speech, questions can be formed by adding a **question tag**.

> You will help, won't you?

Commands

Commands instruct the reader to do something. They usually start with a verb.

> Visit the greatest show on Earth.   Fold the sheet of paper in half.
>
> Try out these tricks on your friends.   Have fun playing this game.

Exclamations

Exclamations are short sentences that express emotion, such as surprise. Lots of exclamations start with the words 'What' or 'How'. For example:

> What a surprise!   How silly!

Test yourself

Write a statement, a question, a command and an exclamation that you could use in an advertisement for ice cream.

Remember

Use different types of sentence in your writing: statements, questions, commands, exclamations.

Adverbs and adverbials

You can add an **adverb** or **adverbial** to a sentence to give additional information about an event. The adverb or adverbial might say how, when or where the event takes place. When you write, adverbials help you to include more detail in a sentence.

Adverbs

Many adverbs describe how, but some tell you where, when or how often. For example:

She quickly picked up the box.   *how it was done*

She carefully picked up the box.

She picked up the box yesterday.   *when it was done*

She picked up the box outside.   *where it was done*

She never picked up the box.   *how often it was done*

Adverbials

An adverbial works like an adverb. It gives extra information about the event. Many adverbials are **phrases** that start with a **preposition**. For example:

She picked up the box after breakfast.   *when*

She picked up the box from the table.   *where*

She picked up the box with some effort.   *how*

Fronting adverbials

Adverbs and adverbials can often be moved to the beginning of a sentence. This is useful when writing because it helps to vary sentence openings. It also draws attention to the detail given in the adverbial. For example:

Carefully, she picked up the box.   *emphasises how she picked it up*

After breakfast, she picked up the box.   *clearly signals when it happened*

Other uses of adverbs

Adverbs can also be used to comment on events, show possibility or add shades of meaning.

Unfortunately, the discovery came too late.   *adds a comment*

Perhaps he will come later.   *shows it's a possibility*

He was extremely late.   *emphasises how late*

Test yourself

1. Find the two adverbs in this sentence.

   Jade carefully lifted the latch and slipped quietly through the gate.

2. Now rewrite the sentence so that it begins with the first adverb. Remember to use any punctuation needed.

Remember

Adverbs and adverbials add information about the event in a sentence.

Expanded noun phrases

You can add more detail about a **noun** by adding other words to it. Adding a **determiner**, **adjectives**, other nouns or a **prepositional phrase** creates an expanded noun phrase.

These noun phrases help you describe things, adding detail to make your writing precise and accurate, as well as more interesting.

Adding determiners and other nouns

A determiner is the little word that goes directly before the noun, such as 'a', 'the', 'some'. It can help you be more exact about which noun you are referring to. For example:

She picked up a box.   ←—— *any* **box**

She picked up the box.   ←—— *a known* **box**

She picked up this box...   that box...   her box.   ←—— *exactly* which **box**

You could also add another noun to be even more precise. For example:

She picked up her jewellery box.

She picked up the toy box.

Adding prepositional phrases

You can add a prepositional phrase after the noun to give more detail and create an even clearer picture. Prepositional phrases start with prepositions. For example:

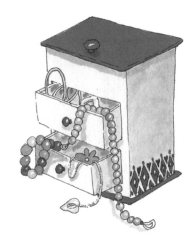

She picked up the jewellery box with the red lid.

Adding adjectives

An adjective is a word that describes or gives more information about a noun. You can add adjectives before or after the noun.

He had a pleasant, friendly face.

His face was red and angry.

Adjectives are important because they help to describe and create effects. For example, the adjectives chosen here create two very different scenes and different moods.

Leo looked up at the grey, angry sky.

Leo looked up at the glorious blue sky.

Always choose adjectives carefully. Don't use too many – just one or two that add something important. Think about the picture or effect you want to create.

Test yourself

Rewrite these sentences, expanding all the nouns into noun phrases.
1. The child walked down the street.
2. The children came to a house.
3. A man watched the sea.

Remember

A precise expanded noun phrase might include a determiner, noun, adjective(s) and/or prepositional phrase.

Conjunctions and subordinate clauses

You can make a single-**clause** sentence longer by adding a **subordinate clause**. The original sentence is the main clause because it makes sense on its own. The subordinate clause expands on the idea or says more about the event. It does not make sense on its own.

You can start a subordinate clause with a **conjunction** such as 'when', 'as', 'because', 'until'. For example:

She picked up the box when it was empty.   ← *subordinate clause – this is added to the main clause (or original sentence) and does not make sense by itself*

main clause – this makes sense on its own

Using subordinating conjunctions

Subordinating conjunctions link subordinate clauses to main clauses. There are many conjunctions you can use to introduce subordinate clauses.

after	as	although	before	because	while	whenever
since	if	unless	until	though	when	while/whilst

Choosing the right conjunction

You must use the right conjunction to link the ideas together. For example, think about how these two ideas might link together:

The houses were made of wood.   The fire spread quickly.

Here there is a cause and effect, so you need a conjunction like 'because', 'as' or 'so'.

As the houses were made of wood, the fire spread quickly.

The fire spread quickly because the houses were made of wood.

The houses were made of wood so the fire spread quickly.

Other conjunctions link ideas in different ways. For example:

We went outside after the rain stopped.   ← *adds a time link*

Entry will be free if you arrive early.   ← *adds a condition*

He lived quite simply even though he was extremely rich.   ← *links two contrasting ideas*

Test yourself

Choose a suitable conjunction from those shown to complete this sentence.

The fire-fighters continued to fight the blaze **although** they were exhausted.

because   if   although   as   since

Remember

Choose the correct conjunctions to introduce subordinate clauses in your sentences.

Relative clauses

A **relative clause** is a special type of **subordinate clause**. It often begins with a **relative pronoun** such as 'who', 'which', 'whose', 'that'.

Relative clauses often come directly after **nouns** to make clear exactly which person, place or thing the sentence is about.

> It was the boy **who** lived in the next village.
>
> They questioned the old lady **whose** bag was stolen.
>
> They visited the street **where** Tilly was last seen.
>
> I found the letter **that** she wrote yesterday in the bin.

Sometimes a relative clause refers to the event in the sentence rather than the noun. In this example, the relative clause comes at the end of the sentence after the **verb**.

> The gates were locked, **which** was surprising. ← *refers to the event of the gates being locked*

Embedding relative clauses

Relative clauses can also be used to add extra detail about someone or something into the middle of a sentence. This extra detail is embedded in (or dropped into) the sentence after the noun.

> Rowan, **who** knew this was his last chance, took a deep breath.
>
> Yasmin, **whose** hands were shaking, opened the box.
>
> The dragon, **which** was breathing plumes of smoke, opened its leathery wings.

In sentences like this, commas are used to separate the extra detail from the main sentence. (Read more about this on pages 51 and 54.)

Leaving out relative pronouns

Sometimes the relative pronoun can be left out and the sentence will still make sense.

> The cake ~~that~~ I chose was delicious.
>
> Harriet, ~~who is~~ Mayam's mother, was quickly on the scene.
>
> The dragon, ~~which was~~ breathing plumes of smoke, opened its leathery wings.

Test yourself

Write this information as one sentence, using a relative clause. Remember the punctuation.

Sophie was desperate to escape. Sophie was breathing rapidly.

Remember

Use relative clauses to add important or helpful details into sentences.

More subordinate clauses

Once you know how to construct sentences with subordinate clauses you can use them to expand on ideas, link pieces of information and express your thoughts more clearly. Here are some more sentence structures that you may find useful.

Multi-clause sentences

A sentence can have more than two clauses. Using a longer sentence can help make your writing flow and sound better. For example, here is part of a story written in single-clause sentences.

> Annie followed the path. She came to a gate. The gate was padlocked.

The short sentences sound jerky but this could be rewritten as one sentence.

> Annie followed the path until she came to a gate, which was padlocked.

When you are writing, think in sentences and say each one in your head. Try different ways of forming the sentence. Rehearsing sentences like this means that you can try out different versions of the sentence and listen for which version sounds best.

Starting with subordinate clauses

Subordinate clauses can be placed at the start of sentences. This helps add variety to your sentences. It can also help draw attention to the detail that is given in the subordinate clause.

> If you leave it too long, **the paint will dry.**   ◄——— *draws attention to the warning*

> Although his hands shook, **he lifted the lid.**   ◄——— *draws attention to his feelings*

Try moving a subordinate clause to the start of a sentence. Think about the effect and decide which version sounds best.

Clauses with –ing or –ed

Not all subordinate clauses start with a **conjunction** or relative pronoun. Sometimes they start with a verb. This can be another effective way of opening a sentence.

> **Whistling** happily to herself, **she strolled around the garden.**

> **Hearing** the alarm, **they rushed outside.**

> **Annoyed** by the decision, **he resigned immediately.**

Notice how commas are used when sentences start with subordinate clauses (see page 51).

Test yourself

Add a subordinate clause to the start of these sentences.
1. He stepped onto the stage
2. She climbed down.

Remember

Sentences can start with subordinate clauses. Try saying different versions of a sentence to see the effect.

Linking adverbials

Linking **adverbials** are words and **phrases** that help link together ideas in a text. They help to achieve **cohesion**.

While **conjunctions** link ideas within a sentence, these adverbials link ideas in different sentences or paragraphs. They usually (though not always) appear at the start of sentences or paragraphs to show how events or ideas follow on.

You should use a range of adverbials to show how your ideas link together.

Time adverbials

These adverbials show time relationships between events. For example, when writing stories, accounts and some explanations:

Just then,...	Later that day,...	In the end,...	Afterwards,...	At that moment,...
Earlier,...	Until then,...	Prior to this,...	Meanwhile,...	At the same time,...

Cause-and-effect adverbials

These adverbials show how one event causes or results in something else. For example, when explaining ideas in reports, persuasive texts and discussions, try using:

Consequently,...   As a result,...   Therefore,...   Because of this,...   As a consequence,...

Contrast adverbials

These adverbials introduce an idea different to the one before. For example, when writing comparisons or discussions, try using:

However,...   In contrast,...   On the other hand,...   Despite this,...

Place adverbials

These adverbials signal movements in place, such as a change of setting or focus. For example:

Outside,...   In other countries,...   On the other side of...

Number or order adverbials

These adverbials help you to present a list of ideas or a series of points. For example:

First of all,...	Firstly,...	Secondly,...
Thirdly,...	Lastly,...	Finally,...

Test yourself

Choose the adverbial that correctly links the two ideas in these sentences. Remember to use any punctuation needed.

Mobile phones can be very useful. _____ some people find them annoying.

Later   Therefore   However

Remember

Use a range of adverbials to show how ideas in different sentences and paragraphs link together.

Verb tenses: past and present

Writing can be in the past **tense** or present tense. Past tense describes things that have already happened; present tense describes things as they are now.

You need to select the right tense for different types of writing. For example, stories are usually in the past tense, while an explanation of how something works would be in the present tense. Tense is shown through the correct use of **verb** forms.

Past and present forms

For many verbs, tense is shown by the verb ending because the past tense form usually ends with –ed.

I follow ⟶ I follow**ed**   they pull ⟶ they pull**ed**   he sighs ⟶ he sigh**ed**

(Note that present tense verbs end –s after 'he', 'she', 'it' or a singular **noun**.)

Some verbs have a different word for the past tense. Here are some examples, but you can probably think of many others.

| take ⟶ took | leave ⟶ left | find ⟶ found | eat ⟶ ate | write ⟶ wrote |
| go ⟶ went | drink ⟶ drank | break ⟶ broke | give ⟶ gave | do ⟶ did |

Past and present progressive forms

The progressive or –ing form of a verb is used when an action is (or was) in progress. It is formed with 'am', 'is' and 'are' in the present tense and with 'was' or 'were' in the past tense.

We are working on an idea. (present) ⟶ We were working on an idea. (past)

Someone is following me. (present) ⟶ Someone was following me. (past)

Perfect forms

Sometimes you need to refer to an event that happened before or earlier on. You can do this by using an additional verb before the main verb. Use 'have' or 'has' in the present tense and 'had' in the past tense.

They have gone out, so I am all alone.

Rosie has arrived already – she is over there.

He had been ill but was better now.

By the time we arrived, he had left.

More verb forms

Other **verb** forms use additional verbs before the main verbs. For example, if you want to write about something in the future you can use the additional verb 'will'.

We will stop soon.   We will leave at ten.   I will have finished by six o'clock.

Or you can use the verb chain 'am/is/are going to'.

We are going to leave at ten.   She is going to stop soon.

There are other verb forms that can help you to express ideas clearly.

Modal verbs – possibility

Modal verbs are verbs like 'might', 'would', 'must', 'should'. They can be used with other verbs to show how likely something is to happen. For example, look at how the modal verbs change the meaning of this sentence.

His invention might work.   It could work.   It should work.   It will work.

Modal verbs show different levels of possibility. 'Might' sounds not very likely but 'will' sounds certain. Modal verbs like these are useful when making predictions, discussing possibilities or considering ideas to show which are more or less likely.

Active and passive verbs

Active sentences usually start with the **subject** (the 'doer' of the action) followed by the verb or action performed. Sometimes there is also an **object** (the person or thing affected by the action). For example:

Sarah hid the picture.   ⟵—— *subject = Sarah; object = the picture*

But sometimes you might deliberately change the focus of the sentence by making the object of the sentence into the subject. To do this you need to use the **passive** form of the verb. For example:

The picture was hidden [by Sarah].   ⟵—— *the original subject (Sarah) can be added on the end or left out completely*

Test yourself

Find the modal verb in each of these sentences. Which of these events is most likely to happen?

1. This might solve the problem.
2. They will be here soon.
3. It should be warm in summer.
4. I could go to the library.

Remember

Think about the effect of using modal verbs or passives in sentences.

Pronouns

A **pronoun** is a word used in place of a **noun**. The pronouns used most often are personal pronouns such as 'I', 'you', 'she', 'him', 'us', 'it'. There are also possessive pronouns such as 'my', 'your', 'ours', 'theirs'. Using these pronouns means that you do not need to keep repeating the same names or nouns throughout a text.

Here is an example to show why pronouns are used:

Olivia lost Olivia's phone but then Olivia found Olivia's phone.

Olivia lost her phone but then she found it.

In the second sentence, pronouns replace some of the nouns. The sentence sounds much better. Be careful, though – too many pronouns and your reader will become confused.

Avoiding ambiguity

When using pronouns, always make sure it is clear who or what you are talking about. Sometimes you need to repeat the name or noun to avoid any **ambiguity** and help the reader follow the meaning. Always reread sentences and paragraphs to check that it is clear who or what the pronouns refer to.

Olivia lost Mia's phone but then ~~she~~ Mia found it.

Using pronouns for cohesion

Pronouns also make links between sentences and help give your writing **cohesion**.

Indira decided to stay on the beach. It was not a good idea, as she soon discovered.

refers to the decision to stay on the beach   refers to Indira

The pronouns in the second sentence refer back to words or ideas in the first sentence. The second sentence would not make sense without the first. You need to go back and read the previous sentence to find out what and who is being referred to. When you are writing it is important to check that these links are clear.

Test yourself

Rewrite these sentences using pronouns to replace some of the nouns.

Amy put the hat on. The hat was too big and fell over Amy's eyes. 'The hat can't be Amy's,' thought Amy. 'The hat must be Ed's.'

Remember

Pronouns are useful for cohesion and to avoid repeating nouns – but make sure it is clear who or what they refer to.

Checking your grammar

There is a lot to think about when you are writing. That is why it is important to keep rereading, checking and **editing** your writing. Once you have finished writing, always read through your work to check the grammar. Read aloud in your head and check that everything is clear and sounds right.

Here is a checklist of grammatical errors to look for.

Verbs and tense

- Check that the correct **tense** is used throughout the piece of writing. It is easy to slip from one tense to another halfway through, so check this and put it right.

- Correct any non-standard **verb** forms that may have slipped into your writing. Write the correct word to replace the error.

    We ~~seen~~ saw the man.   He ~~done~~ did it.   He ~~feeled~~ felt the edge.

- Make sure that **subjects** and verbs agree. Remember some verbs or verb endings change depending on the subject. For example:

    the wolf hunts ——➤ wolves hunt

    he was waiting ——➤ they were waiting

    I am angry ——➤ we are angry

Word class

Check for words that sound wrong. Think about what the correct word should be.
For example:

    He played ~~superb~~ all match.   ◄—— *should be an* **adverb** *– superbly*

    They were the ~~more~~ stronger team.   ◄—— *should just be* '*stronger*' *or* '*much stronger*'

Confusing words

Here are some more words that are often confused. Make sure you use the correct **Standard English** word.

- a or an? Use 'a' before a word starting with a **consonant** and 'an' before a word that starts with a **vowel**.

    a peg   an egg

- I or me? Use 'I' for the subject of the sentence and 'me' for the **object**.

    Tess and I went home.   Lou sent the gift to Tess and me.

- good or well? Use 'good' as an **adjective** and 'well' as an adverb.

    He is a good swimmer.   He swam well.

- those or them? Use 'those' as a **determiner** and 'them' as a **pronoun**.

    Look at those shoes.   Just look at them.

Test yourself

Find the two grammatical errors in this sentence and write the corrections.

The manager weren't sure if they would work good as a team.

(wasn't) (well)

Remember

Check and edit your writing. Make sure the tense is consistent and that subjects and verbs agree. Correct any grammatical errors.

Word classes: revision

When you are reading and writing it is important to understand the different **word classes** (**nouns**, **verbs**, **adjectives**, **adverbs**, **conjunctions**, **pronouns**, **prepositions** and **determiners**) and how they work together. If you have worked through the Grammar topics in this book you should be familiar with these terms.

The examples below will help you with some of the tricky terms that often cause confusion.

Which word class?

Words are grouped into word classes. These word classes tell you how words are used. For example:

- verbs tell us actions
- adverbs tell us how these actions are performed.

Be careful, though. You cannot just look at a word and guess its word class. You need to think about how the word is used in the given sentence. The examples below show why this is important.

Adverb confusions

Adverbs often end with −ly, but think about how the words in blue are used in these sentences. Which is the adverb?

It was a lovely meal.   ⟵ *adjective – it describes the meal (noun)*

He ran fast.   ⟵ *adverb – it describes how he ran (verb)*

Same word, different class

The same word can belong in a different word class in different sentences. You must think about how the word is used in the sentence you are given. For example:

They drive to the shops.   ⟵ *verb – it tells you the action*

They park on the drive.   ⟵ *noun – it names a place*

Words like 'his', 'her', 'my' are possessive pronouns but they can also be used as a determiner before the noun. Look at how the word 'her' is used in this sentence.

I looked in her bag.   ⟵ *determiner for 'bag' – it helps to identify which bag*

Words like 'when', 'after', 'until', 'since' can be prepositions or conjunctions – it all depends on how they are used in a sentence. It is a conjunction if it is followed by a **clause** (with a verb). It is a preposition when followed by a noun or noun **phrase** (no verb). For example:

I helped Dad before I went to school.   ⟵ *conjunction – it introduces a clause*

I saw him before morning break.   ⟵ *preposition – it starts an **adverbial** phrase*

Test yourself

Read this sentence. Write the word class of each word shown in blue.

Some joggers went for a run after breakfast.

Remember

To work out the word class, always think about how the word is used in that sentence.

Synonyms

Synonyms are words with the same or similar meanings. Many words used every day have a number of synonyms. This is very useful to you as a writer because you can replace an everyday word with a more interesting or precise synonym. Try collecting synonyms for **verbs** and **adjectives** you use often in your writing.

run	sprint, race, dash, dart, jog, gallop
strange	odd, peculiar, curious, bizarre, weird, abnormal
great	superb, marvellous, tremendous, fabulous, fantastic

When you are writing or **editing**, refer to these lists and select synonyms to use. There is no need to keep repeating a word when you can use a good alternative.

Using a thesaurus

A **thesaurus** provides lists of synonyms for lots of words. Use a thesaurus to help widen your choice of words so you make more interesting and adventurous choices. When editing, use a thesaurus to help replace words with more precise or effective synonyms.

Greenville is a well-off an affluent area.

The bridge looked shaky precarious.

She is a shady suspicious character.

Shades of meaning

Synonyms do not all have exactly the same meaning. You need to choose the synonym that best expresses what you are trying to say or that creates the effect you want. Try a few synonyms in the sentence to see which best expresses your meaning or effect.

He drank the milk.	He sipped… gulped… guzzled the milk.
a dark room	a dull… dingy… shadowy room

Be careful when you choose. It is important to find a synonym that makes sense in your sentence. For example, which synonym would fit best in these sentences?

He had a high voice. ⟵ *towering, lofty or shrill?*

It was an old manuscript. ⟵ *elderly, mature or ancient?*

Test yourself

Replace the words in blue with suitable synonyms.

I was feeling quite worried when I saw the terrible weather.

Remember

Synonyms are words with similar meanings. Select a synonym that makes your meaning clearer or adds to the effect you want to create.

Antonyms

Antonyms are words with opposite meanings. Many words have opposites. For example:

rich — poor   loud — quiet   liquid — solid   float — sink   war — peace

Some words have more than one antonym because they have more than one meaning.

light — dark (blue)

light — heavy (load)

light — extinguish (the fire)

clear — cloudy (liquid)

clear — confusing (instructions)

clear — blocked (road)

Forming antonyms with prefixes

Some antonyms are formed by adding **prefixes** such as un–, dis–, in–. These prefixes mean 'not' so when they are added to words they create words with opposite meanings.

unworthy	uneven	dishonest	discomfort	inaccurate
informal	impossible	impatient	illegible	irrelevant

im–, il–, ir– are all forms of the prefix in–

When these prefixes are added to verbs they create words that mean the opposite or reverse.

uncover   unlock   decode   disassemble   dislodge   discontinue

Using antonyms

Pairs of antonyms can be useful if you want to show contrasts.

Holly was getting quite tall while Ella was still rather short.

As the prices increased, the number of customers decreased.

They looked like a professional team while we were just amateurs.

Shades of meaning

Antonyms are opposites but between any pair of antonyms there can be a whole range of words with different shades of meaning.

sad ➞ happy: dejected ➞ miserable ➞ glum ➞ glad ➞ delighted ➞ ecstatic

wet ➞ dry: saturated ➞ drenched ➞ moist ➞ damp ➞ dry ➞ parched

Test yourself

Write an antonym for each of these words.
1. obey
2. perfect
3. forwards
4. inflate
5. trivial
6. succeed

Remember

Antonyms are words with opposite meanings. You can often form antonyms by adding 'opposite' prefixes.

Sentence punctuation

The start of a sentence must be clearly shown with a capital letter and the end with a full stop (or a question mark or exclamation mark, if appropriate). If you think in sentences as you write, then you will get into the habit of using sentence punctuation as you go.

Writing in sentences

As you write each sentence, start it with a capital letter and end it with a full stop. If you write a question or an exclamation, remember to put a question mark or an exclamation mark instead of a full stop.

use a capital letter *at the start of a sentence*

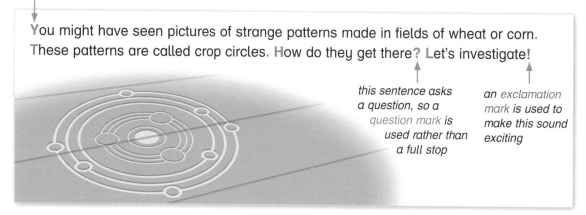

You might have seen pictures of strange patterns made in fields of wheat or corn. These patterns are called crop circles. How do they get there? Let's investigate!

this sentence asks a question, so a question mark *is used rather than a full stop*

an exclamation mark is used to make this sound exciting

Proofreading

Once you have finished your writing, it is important to **proofread** your work. Check that you have correctly punctuated the start and end of sentences. Read aloud in your head, so that you can hear where each sentence ends. A common mistake is to use commas to separate sentences rather than full stops, like this:

> She shouted and shouted but no-one heard, perhaps there was no-one left to hear, the silence closed in around her.

This is wrong. Full stops rather than commas are needed here to separate out the three sentences, like this:

> She shouted and shouted but no-one heard. Perhaps there was no-one left to hear. The silence closed in around her.

Capital letters

Capital letters are also used for:

- proper **nouns** – names of people, places, days of the week, months of the year
- titles – people (Mrs, Dr, Sir), organisations, films, books, television programmes
- making a word stand out – 'HELP!'

Test yourself

Proofread this extract. Add the missing sentence punctuation.

many people keep animals as pets cats and dogs are particularly popular other people prefer smaller animals such as gerbils or hamsters which do you prefer

Remember

Punctuate each sentence as you write it. Check that it has a capital letter and a full stop – or else '?' or '!'.

Commas

Commas are used within a sentence. They show the breaks between different parts of the sentence such as **phrases** or **clauses**. They are important because they help to make the meaning of the sentence clear to the reader.

Separating items in a list

Use commas between items in a list of nouns or noun phrases, or in sentences with a list of **verbs** or **adjectives**.

> In the wooden box there was an old-fashioned fountain pen, some coins, a matchbox and a folded piece of paper.

> It was a thin, grey, hungry dog.

no comma before the 'and' at the end of a list – there is no need for one

After fronted adverbs or adverbials

Use a comma when a sentence starts with an **adverb** or **adverbial**.

> Outside, snow fell steadily. Excitedly, the children watched it.

> After a long time, he came to the end.

> With a heavy heart, he trudged home.

Marking embedded words, phrases or clauses

Use two commas to mark off additional words, phrases or clauses dropped into the middle of a sentence.

> Ken, a former pilot, was a reluctant hero.

> It was, however, a big mistake.

After fronted subordinate clauses

Use a comma if a **subordinate clause** is placed at the start of a sentence.

> While the dough is rising, heat the oven to the correct temperature.

> Smiling nervously at her guests, she opened the door.

Clarifying meaning

Use a comma in any sentence where it helps to make the meaning clear.

> Are you ready to eat, Luca?

> Erin, James is waiting.

> She was not ready, yet it was time to begin.

Test yourself

Insert the missing comma or commas into these sentences.

1. Mr Roberts my teacher is very strange.
2. First sieve the flour into the bowl.
3. Although it was very late we were wide awake.

Remember

Use commas within sentences to separate phrases and clauses, and to make your meaning clear.

Direct speech

The layout and punctuation of **direct speech** help the reader follow who is saying what. Inverted commas or speech marks go at the start and end of the spoken words, to separate the spoken words from the reporting **clause** (the rest of the sentence). A new line is started each time a different person starts to speak.

'Where have you been?' demanded Leah.
'I said six o'clock.'
'Sorry, I just couldn't get away,' sighed Abby.
'Well it's too late now, isn't it?
They've already gone,' complained Leah.
'Sorry,' repeated Abby sadly.

Commas in direct speech

A comma is used to separate the spoken words from the reporting clause. The comma goes inside the inverted commas, like this:

'I couldn't get away,' sighed Abby.

You can switch the sentence round and start with the reporting clause. The comma then goes at the end of the reporting clause, with a full stop at the end of the spoken words, like this:

Abby said, 'Sorry I'm late.'

End punctuation

If someone asks a question or says something with strong feeling, the question mark or exclamation mark also goes inside the inverted commas, like this:

'Over here!' shouted Toby.
'Where have you been?' demanded Leah. 'I said six o'clock.'

The first letter inside the inverted commas is nearly always a capital letter. Only start with a lower case letter if a speech is interrupted in the middle of a sentence.

Test yourself

Add the punctuation needed in this dialogue.

Where are you Kris shouted.

I'm over here, behind the fireplace. There's some sort of secret tunnel said a muffled voice.

How did you get in there asked Kris, feeling around the fireplace for a lever or handle.

Remember

Put inverted commas round any spoken words, with the comma or other end punctuation placed *inside* the inverted commas.

Apostrophes

There are two types of apostrophe: the apostrophe used in contractions or shortened words and the apostrophe used to show possession. These are sometimes called apostrophes for omission and apostrophes for possession.

Apostrophes for omission

This apostrophe is used in contractions, the shortened form of **verbs** often used in **informal** speech and writing.

    it's (it is)   haven't (have not)   she'll (she will)

To use this type of apostrophe correctly, imagine that the two words are written in full. In the contraction or shortened form, one or more letters are missing. The apostrophe goes where the missing letter(s) would be.

You might use this apostrophe when you are writing direct speech in a story, or in an informal, chatty letter:

    I'm sure he'll understand if you're a bit late.

Apostrophes for possession

The possessive apostrophe is used to show that something belongs to someone or something. The –'s ('apostrophe s') is added onto the **noun** or name of the owner, like this:

    the tiger's stripes   Michael's party   all the king's horses

When there are plural owners, the rules are a little more complicated. If the plural noun already ends with –s, then just the apostrophe is added after the –s, like this:

    his parents' house   the teachers' staffroom

But if the plural version of the noun does not end with –s, then add –'s, like this:

    the children's playroom   the men's changing room

Be careful!

Don't use apostrophes anywhere else. Don't use –'s for normal plural endings. Don't use apostrophes in possessive **pronouns** such as 'its' or 'yours'.

    This is yours.   The tree has lost its leaves.

Test yourself

Insert the missing apostrophes into these sentences.
1. The twins wont go to Amelias house.
2. The jugglers wouldnt laugh at Coco the clowns tricks.

Remember

Use apostrophes in contractions (to show there are missing letters) or to show possession. Don't use them anywhere else!

Parenthesis: brackets, dashes, commas

Sometimes an extra word, **phrase** or **clause** is added into the middle of a sentence. This is called a **parenthesis**. It is a simple way of adding extra information into a sentence. The extra information must be clearly separated from the main sentence using brackets, dashes or commas. There are no very strict rules about which of these to use. The best way to learn is to look out for examples of parenthesis as you read.

Using brackets

Brackets are always used as a pair. The extra information goes inside the brackets. The brackets very clearly separate the extra information from the main sentence.

> The twins (Sam and Josh) were late.

> I wrote to Mrs Manson (the manager) with my complaint.

Using dashes

A pair of dashes can be used in the same way as brackets. The extra phrase or piece of information that has been dropped into the sentence goes between the two dashes.

> The children – as always – were late.

> It was a glorious day – bright sunshine, in fact – so we went swimming.

> She chose a hat – a big, floppy sunhat – from the pile.

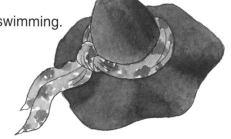

You can also use a single dash to add an extra piece of information onto the end of a sentence. This is often used for effect or surprise, as it helps to create a dramatic pause:

> Grandad cooked us a meal – it was terrible!

> I tried the key in the lock – it worked!

> I was quietly watching TV when – CRASH!

Using commas

A pair of commas can be used in the same way as brackets or a pair of dashes. Commas usually make your writing smoother than brackets or dashes. For example:

> The twins, Sam and Josh, were late.

> I spoke to Mrs Manson, the manager, about my complaint.

You can use this technique in all sorts of writing – stories, news reports and more **formal** writing.

Test yourself

Add commas, brackets or dashes in the correct place in these sentences.
1. Mr Hawkins the head teacher wrote to all the parents.
2. For dinner, it was sprouts yuk and shepherd's pie.
3. Kevin smiling broadly stepped onto the stage.

Remember

Use brackets, or a pair of dashes or commas, to separate the extra information dropped into the middle of a sentence.

Colons and semi-colons

Colons and **semi-colons** are usually found in more formal writing and writing aimed at older readers or an adult audience. Using colons and semi-colons in your writing can help make your writing more formal and seem more mature.

Colons and semi-colons are used in two different ways.

Writing in lists

A colon is used to introduce a list of items in a sentence.

> He unpacked his lunch: sandwiches, a slice of cake, crisps and an apple.

A colon can also be used if a list sentence is turned into bullet points.

> Lunch included these items:
> - sandwiches
> - a slice of cake
> - crisps
> - an apple.

Semi-colons are used in lists made up of longer **phrases**, which may already include commas. The semi-colons separate the items in the list:

> The mouse had tiny, beady eyes; perfectly formed pink ears; curiously twitching whiskers and a most inquisitive look.

Separating clauses

Colons and semi-colons can be used to link two main clauses within a sentence. The colon or semi-colon goes between the two clauses.

A colon can introduce a second part of a sentence that explains, illustrates or gives more information about the first part of the sentence.

> It was too late: the tide had turned.

A semi-colon works like a **conjunction** linking two closely connected main clauses.

> Mohammed was clever and worked hard; David was lazy and easily bored.

In **informal** writing, a dash is sometimes used in the same way (see page 54).

(see page 54)

Test yourself

Insert a colon or semi-colon in the correct place in these sentences.
1. The days were hot and dry the nights were very cold.
2. We had one chance find the missing key.
3. They divided the books into three piles fiction, non-fiction and poetry.
4. Some people were amazed some were horrified.

Remember

Use colons and semi-colons in lists or between clauses in a sentence.

Punctuation for meaning and effect

Punctuation is important because it helps the reader to follow the meaning of a piece of writing. It also gives the reader important clues about how the text should sound when it is read aloud. **Proofread** your writing by reading it aloud in your head so you can hear where punctuation is needed to make the meaning clear or for effect.

It is difficult to read something with no punctuation.

> Caitlin Brown are you with us Mrs Andersons voice cut into my comfortable dream world it was a hot afternoon too hot for history projects

Without punctuation, you do not know where to pause or what expression to use. Punctuation makes it easier to read and gives you an idea what expression to use.

> 'Caitlin Brown! Are you with us?' Mrs Anderson's voice cut into my comfortable dream world. It was a hot afternoon – too hot for history projects.

Clarifying meaning

Punctuation is sometimes essential to make your meaning clear and to avoid **ambiguity** or confusion. Read these sentences with and without punctuation. Can you see why the comma and **hyphen** are needed?

He hates lazy people like you.
↑
you are lazy

He hates lazy people, like you.
↑
he agrees with you

I find Tim a little big headed.
↑
just confusing!

I find Tim a little big-headed.
↑
a bit conceited

Hyphens are used to show which words go together. For example:

he is big-headed   she is absent-minded   he was red-faced

Punctuation for effect

Punctuation can also be used for effect. It can help to bring your writing to life. Think about how you want your writing to sound and how punctuation can help achieve this effect.

> Ever dreamed of being a Grand Prix driver? Well, here's your chance. The new GP Driver game puts you – yes you! – behind the wheel. It's fast, it's furious… it's FUN, FUN, FUN!

An ellipsis (…) is used to show that something is incomplete. It is often used to create a dramatic effect. For example:

> The door creaked on its rusty hinges and swung slowly open…

Test yourself

Insert the missing hyphen in the sentence below. Why is it needed?

He defeated the evil wizard, the three witches and the terrible man eating monsters.

Remember

Use punctuation to make your meaning clear – and for effect!

Learning to spell words

Knowing how to spell is important. Correct spelling makes your writing easier to read. Being able to spell words easily also allows you to focus more on what you are writing, rather than how you spell it. It is especially important to learn to spell words that you often use in your writing, or those you often get wrong.

To learn to spell a difficult word you need to look at it very carefully. Some of the word is likely to be quite straightforward but there is probably an unusual spelling somewhere in it. You need to find this tricky part and remember it.

It can sometimes help to write the word a number of times, or to say the word how it is spelt. You might use a **mnemonic** to help you. Try all of these methods and see what works best for you.

Finding the tricky part

Try these steps.

1. Look at the word carefully, say it and highlight the tricky part. That's the part you need to remember.

    favourite   rhyme   ancient

2. Cover the word. Picture it in your head.

3. Write it without looking at the covered word. Does it look right?

4. Uncover the word and check that you have spelt it right.

Using mnemonics

You might find that a mnemonic helps you to remember the tricky part of a spelling.

cemetery ⟶ all the **vowel letters** in the cemetery are 'e's

secretary ⟶ a **secret secret**ary

address ⟶ **add** your **add**ress

rhythm ⟶ **r**hythm **h**as **y**our **t**wo **h**ips **m**oving

Learning letter strings

Some letter strings are found in many words. If you learn to spell one word you could learn other words at the same time.

thought	brought	although	enough	through	cough	plough

usual	actual	casual	manual	factual	individual	virtual

Test yourself

Use the ideas on this page to help you learn to spell these words.

1. thorough
2. foreign
3. soldier
4. persuade
5. shoulder
6. queue
7. yacht
8. amateur

Remember

Identify the tricky part of a word and find a way of remembering it.

Spelling longer words

When you are spelling longer words, it is a good idea to break them into **syllables**. You can then think about each part of the word separately, rather than the whole word altogether.

In some longer words, there is a hidden or unstressed letter or syllable, which is difficult to hear when the word is said normally. By saying the word as separate syllables you reveal these hidden letters. This will help you to spell the word correctly.

Syllable by syllable

Some words are easier to spell if you break them up into syllables.

re/mem/ber/ing	im/por/tant	ca/len/dar
ex/pe/ri/ment	dif/fi/cult	ma/te/ri/al

Hidden letters

Sometimes breaking words up into syllables helps you find hidden or unstressed letters.

math/e/ma/tics	choc/o/late	se/pa/rate
dif/fe/rent	gov/ern/ment	a/ve/rage

You can learn to spell these words by saying them as they are written, rather than as they usually sound. Say the syllables, really stressing the sound of the hidden letter(s).

Feb/ru/a/ry	mis/e/ra/ble	res/tau/rant
in/te/rest/ing	or/di/na/ry	par/tic/u/lar
pop/u/lar	def/i/nite	priv/i/lege

Words within words

Sometimes when you break words down, you can find words within words. This is a useful technique to help you remember how to spell longer words.

re-cog-nise	com-put-er	ve-get-able	ve-hi-cle
com-pet-ition	ex-plan-ation	envi-ron-ment	bar-gain

Test yourself

Copy each word, break it into syllables and underline any hidden vowel sounds.

1. desperate
2. relevant
3. parliament
4. category

Remember

Say the syllables out loud so you can hear unstressed syllables and letters clearly.

Word endings

Spelling word endings can be difficult. Some endings are not spelt as they sound.

–ture	creature, capture, adventure
–sure	measure, treasure, leisure

Some word endings sound the same but have different spellings, so it is difficult to know which one to use.

–able	available, capable, valuable
–ible	possible, horrible, terrible

–cial	special, official, artificial
–tial	partial, confidential, essential

It is important for you to learn to recognise these word endings and which words use them. There are several sets of these confusing endings to learn.

Words ending –ous

This ending is really a **suffix** but there is not always an obvious **root word**. When it follows the letters c or t it makes a different sound.

–ous	tremendous, enormous, jealous, generous
–ious	serious, obvious, curious, previous
–cious	vicious, precious, conscious, suspicious
–tious	ambitious, cautious, fictitious, infectious

Words ending 'shun'

This ending is also a suffix. The root word is usually more obvious, and the end of the root word often gives a clue about whether it is the –t, –s, –ss or –c spelling.

–tion	injection, invention, position, mention
–sion	division, invasion, confusion, decision
–ssion	expression, discussion, possession, profession
–cian	musician, electrician, magician, politician

Other unstressed endings

With unstressed word endings it is difficult to hear the **vowel** sound. Try learning these words by stressing the ending.

–ant/–ent	→	hesitant	independent
–ance/–ence	→	appearance	existence
–ancy/–ency	→	expectancy	frequency
–ary/–ery/–ory	→	dictionary	surgery	history

Test yourself

Add an ending to complete each word.
1. deli____
2. ridicul____
3. nutri____
4. incred____
5. conveni____
6. interfer____

Remember

Learn to spell words that have these tricky word endings.

Adding prefixes and suffixes

Some longer words are **root words** with a **prefix** or **suffix** added. You can spell these words correctly if you know the root, the prefix and/or suffix, and how to add these to the root word.

Adding prefixes

When a prefix is added to the beginning of a root word it does not change the spelling of the root word. Just write the prefix and then the root word. For example:

> dis + appear = disappear   dis + honest = dishonest
> mis + heard = misheard   mis + spell = misspell
> il + logical = illogical   il + legal = illegal
> ir + regular = irregular   ir+ responsible = irresponsible
> re + appear = reappear   re + enter = re-enter

double letter when the prefix ends with the same letter as the word starts

*a **hyphen** is needed when this double letter is two **vowel letters***

Adding suffixes

A suffix is added to the end of a word. This usually changes the **word class**, and sometimes changes the spelling of the root word. In these examples, however, the spelling of the root word does not change.

–ly	completely, finally, frequently
–ful	purposeful, doubtful, successful
–ment	attachment, equipment, development
–ous	poisonous, dangerous, mountainous
–ation	information, recommendation, expectation
–able	comfortable, reasonable, considerable

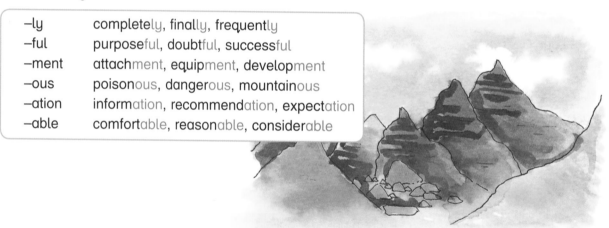

Basic rules for adding suffixes

Here are the main rules for adding suffixes to words ending –e or –y:

Rule 1   For words ending –e, drop the e if the suffix starts with a vowel letter.

> fame + ous = famous   sense + ation = sensation   nature + al = natural

Rule 2   For words ending with a **consonant** and –y, usually, change the y to an i.

> vary + ous = various   rely + able = reliable   naughty + ly = naughtily

Test yourself

Add these prefixes and suffixes to the root words.

1. beauty + ful =
2. early + er =
3. arrive + al =
4. im + mature =
5. dis + heart + en =
6. co + ordinate =

Remember

You can spell a lot of longer words if you know how to add prefixes and suffixes.

Suffix rules and exceptions

The rules for adding suffixes to words ending –e and –y (given on page 60) are very useful. They will help you to spell many words correctly. However, there are some more rules – and some exceptions – that you need to remember when adding suffixes.

Adding –ly

Rule Keep the e when adding –ly to words ending –e.

> extremely   strangely   sincerely

Exceptions Change le to ly if the root word ends –le.

possible → possibly   adorable → adorably   gentle → gently

Other exceptions include: true → truly   whole → wholly

Adding –s

Rule Add –es rather than –s if the plural ending sounds like 'iz' and forms an extra **syllable**, or if the word ends with a consonant and –y.

> address → addresses   library → libraries (y to i rule)

Exceptions Add –es to some words ending *without* an 'iz' sound. For example, some words ending –f or –fe, which change the f to v:

elf → elves   half → halves   knife → knives

And add –es to some words ending o:

potatoes   echoes   heroes

Other exceptions include: fungus → fungi   cactus → cacti

Adding a vowel suffix

Rule 1 Drop the e when adding a vowel suffix to words ending –e.

> breathe → breathing   promise → promised   arrive → arrival

Exceptions Keep the e when adding –able or –ous to words ending –ce or –ge.

manageable   noticeable   courageous

Rule 2 Double the last letter when adding a vowel suffix to words ending with one vowel letter and one consonant letter.

> equipped   forgotten   beginner

Exceptions Don't double the last letter if the last syllable is unstressed.

develop → developed   garden → gardening

With words ending –fer, only double the r if the –fer is still stressed once the ending is added.

prefer → preferred (but preference)

Test yourself

Add these suffixes to the root words.

1. replace + able   3. definite + ly   5. transfer + ed
2. outrage + ous   4. probable + ly   6. refer + ence

Remember

Learn these spelling rules – and the exceptions.

Confusing consonants

Some **consonant** sounds have less common alternative spellings. Some of these spellings are quite unusual, but it is still important to know about them and which words use them.

Unusual spellings

Look out for words with these consonant spellings.

- Words with a 'k' sound spelt ch: chorus, chemist, echo, character, stomach.

- Words with a 'sh' sound spelt ch: chef, chalet, machine, brochure.

- Words with a 's' sound spelt sc: muscle, science, scene, discipline, fascinate, crescent.

- Words with a 'f' sound spelt ph: photograph, phrase, phantom, physical.

- Words ending with a 'g' sound spelt –gue, or a 'k' sound spelt –que: league, vague antique, unique.

's' and 'j' sounds

These two alternative spellings are found in many words.

- A 's' sound is spelt c when it comes before e, i and y:

    bicycle   circle   century   centre   certain   decide   recent   exercise

- A 'j' sound is often spelt g when it comes before e, i and y (but not always):

    general   magic   gym   suggest   imagine   exaggerate

Silent consonant letters

Sometimes consonant sounds have silent letters. You need to know about these in order to spell words correctly. Some common silent letters are:

kn–	knife knight knitting knot knowledge knuckle
wr–	write wrong wrist wrapper wreck wrinkle
–mb	lamb climb crumb plumber numb tomb
–mn	solemn column autumn hymn
–st–	castle whistle wrestle hustle rustle

Test yourself

Complete these words by adding the missing consonant letter.

1. i_land
2. this_le
3. ac_ident
4. ex_ellent
5. ans_er
6. sacrifi_e
7. dou_t
8. pre_udice

Remember

Learn these alternative consonant spellings and which words use them.

Difficult vowels

Vowel sounds often make spelling difficult because in English there are several ways of spelling each sound. For example, the 'er' sound can be spelt er as in 'perhaps', ir as in 'thirty', ur as in 'surprise', ear as in 'earth', or or (after w) as in 'worth'.

You should already know the main spellings for vowel sounds but below are some less common examples.

Unusual spellings

Look out for these unusual vowel spellings.

- Words with the 'i' sound spelt y: myth, Egypt, pyramid, mystery, symbol, crystal
- Words with the 'u' sound spelt ou: young, touch, double, trouble, country
- Words with the 'ay' sound spelt ei or eigh: vein, weight, eight(h), neighbour, sleigh
- Words with the 'oo' or 'yoo' sound spelt ui: fruit, bruise, suit, juice, cruise

ie or ei? – i before e except after c

This is a rule for words where an 'ee' sound is spelt ie or ei. The 'ee' sound is only spelt ei after the letter c.

i before e…			
believe	achieve	fierce	mischief
…except after c			
ceiling	deceive	receive	perceive

Watch out for 'seize' and 'weird', which don't follow this rule!

Silent vowel letters

The letter q is always followed by u (and another vowel letter).

    question, quarter, qualify, quarrel, request, quiet, quick

Also look out for words where g is followed by a silent u.

    guard, guide, guess, guilty, disguise, guitar

Test yourself

Complete these words by adding the missing vowel letter.

1. c_uple
2. s_stem
3. g_arantee
4. sq_irrel
5. nu_sance
6. awkw_rd

Remember

Look out for unusual spellings of vowel sounds and learn them.

Tricky words

Some words are very tricky to spell. Even adults often need to think about them. They might have unusual spellings or confusing letter strings, or they just seem to break all the usual rules. These words need to be learnt.

Once you have learnt to spell a word, use it in your writing. The more times you write a word, the more likely it is that the spelling will stick.

Double and single letters

In some words, the tricky part is remembering if they have double letters. A **mnemonic** can be useful to help you remember words like these. For example:

necessary	⟶ 1 collar; 2 sleeves
accommodate	⟶ 2 caravans and 2 motels
committee	⟶ committees need 2m's, 2t's and 2e's
embarrass	⟶ really red and so shy

Rule breakers

Some words are tricky because the correct spelling doesn't seem right.

   forty (not four-ty)   disastrous (not disaster-ous)

With these words, write the correct spelling a number of times so that it begins to look right.

Finding root words

Sometimes understanding where the word comes from can help you to spell it correctly – perhaps by identifying the **root word**.

   opposite (oppose)   medicine (medic)   business (busy)   criticise (critic)

---

30 tricky words

accompany	community	harass	mischievous	recommend
according	conscience	hindrance	occasion(ally)	signature
aggressive	correspond	immediate(ly)	occurred	sufficient
apparent	curiosity	interrupt	opportunity	temperature
appreciate	determined	language	programme	twelfth
communicate	familiar	marvellous	pronunciation	variety

Test yourself

Use the ideas on pages 57–64 to help you learn how to spell the tricky words in the box.

Remember

Some spellings just need to be learnt. Find a way to help you remember them.

Homophones

Homophones are words that sound the same but are spelt differently and have different meanings. When you write a homophone, you need to know which word is needed.

seen — scene   morning — mourning   rain — rein — reign

With these examples the first word is one you use a lot. The homophones tend to be used for more specialised purposes – for example, you might use 'scene' when writing a play script.

Knowing which is which

The most important thing is to know which spelling has which meaning. Use a dictionary to check the meaning of each spelling in these homophone pairs:

aisle — isle	draft — draught	stationary — stationery
alter — altar	profit — prophet	steel — steal
bridle — bridal	cereal — serial	who's — whose

Using mnemonics

Mnemonics can be useful to help you remember which homophone is which. Here are some homophones that can be confusing – and some helpful mnemonics:

peace (peace is ace)	—	piece (piece of pie)
herd (shepherd)	—	heard (hear with your ear)
meat (you eat meat)	—	meet (two ee's meet)
father (a father might be fat)	—	farther (farther is far off)

Near homophones

Some words are not quite homophones but are so similar that they can still be confusing.

dessert (sweet stuff)	—	desert (only sand)
wary (cautious)	—	weary (tired)
lightning (before thunder)	—	lightening (lighten-ing)

These **verbs** and **nouns** are often confused. Learn which is which.

affect — effect
↑   ↑
verb *noun*

advise — advice
↑   ↑
verb *noun*

devise — device
↑   ↑
verb *noun*

practise — practice
↑   ↑
verb *noun*

Test yourself

Write a homophone for each word.

1. allowed
2. guessed
3. draft
4. led
5. passed

Remember

Think about the meaning of the word you want. Make sure that you write the right homophone.

Deciding what to write

Thinking of an idea is often the hardest part of writing a story. First you need to decide what sort of story you are going to write.

Think about who will read your story and what sort of story they might enjoy. Think about the different types of stories you have read to help you make your choice.

Here are some examples of stories you might write:

- a realistic story set in school or at home
- a fantasy story where characters visit an amazing world
- an adventure story with a danger and exciting events
- a mystery with a puzzle to solve
- a traditional story with a familiar theme and traditional characters.

Borrowing ideas

Once you have decided what type of story you are going to write, think about similar stories you have read. What are the distinctive features of this type of story? What makes them good to read?

You can borrow ideas from these stories to use in your story. Think about the characters, settings, themes and events found in such stories. Think about how the stories begin, how they develop and how they end. What style of story writing is used?

Start to note ideas to use in your story. You might start with an idea for a title, a character, a setting, a theme or an opening event.

Developing your story

Now, you can begin to develop ideas for your story. Use some ideas from stories you have read and add ideas of your own to create your own story.

Decide who and what the story is about. Decide whether the story will be told in the first **person** or third person. Keep making notes as you develop your ideas. For example:

a realistic school story
a shy character... who becomes the centre of attention

Test yourself

You decide to write a fantasy adventure story about a computer game. Note ideas for characters, settings and events in a story like this.

Remember

Think about stories you have read and borrow ideas from them to use in your own story. Add ideas of your own and make notes as you go.

Planning your story

It is important to plan your story before you start writing. You should be clear about the main characters, the setting and what happens in the story. A story is a long piece of writing and having a clear plan will keep you focused as you write. It will help keep the story tight and moving in the right direction.

Make notes about your ideas for characters and settings. Picture them in your head (or make sketches if you have time). Plan all of the events in the story from the opening, right through to the end. You could list the main events or scenes, write them on sticky notes, draw a story map or storyboard, or note your ideas on a flowchart.

A story plan

Here is an example of what your story plan should include. You could use a planning frame like this:

Characters

- Ali – boy – quiet and shy
- Jamie – his friend – outgoing

plan names and key details about main characters, such as their qualities

Setting

- Classroom – busy, building excitement
- School football pitch – excited, cheering, noisy

note a few descriptive words or add notes about atmosphere

Opening

- Ali arrived at school

*plan in note form – use past **tense** for events*

Main events

-
-
-

What happens? What happens next? What happens then? – read more about plotting events on page 68

Ending

-

plan the sequence of events right to the end

Test yourself

Write a plan for the events in your computer game story (see the 'Test yourself' box on page 66). Use a planning frame like the one shown above.

Remember

Make a plan before you start writing. Plan characters, settings and events through to the end, to keep your writing focused.

Structure and plot

The **structure** and plot of your story are very important. A good plot is what keeps readers interested. They want to find out what happens next. It is important to plot the main sequence of events before you begin writing your story. That way you can make sure that the events all link together without any gaps.

Deciding the structure

Thinking about the overall shape or structure of your story will help you to plot a story that works. Think about stories you have read and how those stories were shaped. Some stories are shaped around a journey or a quest. Some are shaped around a problem or threat to be overcome. Some traditional stories have a repeating pattern.

Choose a story pattern that you know well and that works for the story you want to write. Follow the story pattern but add your own characters, settings and events.

Here is an example of a story pattern that you could borrow and adapt.

opening: everything is normal
trigger event: character hears, sees, finds something usual
problem: conflicts, complications, dilemmas caused by the trigger event
climax: danger, disaster seems likely, a threat closes in
resolution: danger avoided, 'problems' solved in a satisfying way
ending: reflect on events

Here is an example of how this story pattern might be used to plot a story.

*out shopping – saw robbery – followed thieves – spotted –
chased – captured – police arrived – rescued – received award*

Plotting the chain of events

Try thinking about the plot as a chain of events, linking all the events together, leading to the end of the story. Each event is one link in the chain. If an important event is missing or weak, then the chain is broken.

the main events

opening — get your reader interested

keep your reader interested

ending — give your reader a satisfying ending

Remember

Choose a story pattern or structure to help you plot the sequence or chain of events in your story.

Narrative voice

Writing a good story is not just about what happens. How you tell the story is just as important. The style or the way you tell your story must hold the reader's attention. Choose a style that fits your story and your audience. There are many different styles of story writing. Think about stories you have read and the different styles used. For example:

the chatty, **informal** style of a realistic story written in the first **person**

the traditional storytelling style of a myth or traditional tale

Once you have chosen a style, keep that 'writer's voice' in your head as you write. Keep reading your story back to see how it sounds when you listen to it as a reader. Does it sound like a story? Does it hold your attention? Have you kept the same writer's voice?

First person stories

When you are writing a story in the first person, you need to take on the 'voice' of the character, as in this example.

> Adam had absolutely no idea about cooking on a camp fire. What a disaster! I told him, there was no way I was eating one of those sausages. They were completely black!

The informal style shows that the story is written in the 'voice' of a child. You can hear the voice in the comments, expression and use of informal words and **phrases**.

Traditional story style

When writing a traditional story you need to use a very different voice. Try imagining and then copying the style of a traditional storyteller. Use the language and rhythms of oral storytelling, including patterned language, and repeated words and phrases.

> And so despite all his brave efforts, the poor unfortunate prince found himself still trapped. Trapped within the four walls of the forgotten castle. No crown, no fortune – and no hope of escape. Or so it seemed…

Different stories, different style

Listen for the style and voice used in different stories you read. Keep examples so you can refer to them before you begin writing your own story. For example, you could collect examples of the descriptive style used in ghost stories.

Test yourself

Write two more sentences for the first person story (above) about the camping trip, using the informal voice of the character.

Remember

Keep reading your writing back to check that you have kept the same style and writer's voice.

Openings and endings

The opening of a story is very important. It needs to introduce the characters, the setting or the subject of the story. But most importantly it needs to capture the reader's interest and make you want to read on. Just starting your story with the words 'One day …', for example, is not going to do this.

There are lots of more interesting or dramatic ways of starting a story.

Starting with description

An interesting description of an important character or setting can help create a mood and intrigue the reader. For example:

> Mrs Donaldson's house was as old and untidy as she was.

> Mrs Donaldson peered at us through the thick lenses of her glasses.

Starting with action

A dramatic event will leave the reader wanting to find out what is happening and why. For example:

> Thud! A box of books fell from the top of the wardrobe onto the dusty floor.

Starting with dialogue

Dialogue can be an interesting way to start a story. It can instantly introduce characters or suggest what the story is about. For example:

> 'Do we have to go?' I pleaded. 'Mrs Donaldson is such a bore.'
> 'Really, Joel! You should be more sympathetic. She's a poor old lady who relies on us for a bit of company,' my sister replied crossly.

Ending effectively

It is also important to give your story a good ending, so as not to disappoint your readers. Once all the problems, complications and mysteries have been solved, make sure you have an ending that ties the story up neatly. Read the last few paragraphs and compose a memorable final sentence.

Try ending with:

- a comment about what happened, reflecting on events
- a question
- a final surprise – or shock
- saying or showing what the main character has learnt
- words spoken by one of the characters
- something referring back to the start of the story – or forward to the future.

Test yourself

Write an effective opening and closing sentence for the computer game story you planned on page 66 (see the 'Test yourself' box).

Remember

Give your story memorable first and last lines.

Using paragraphs

As you write your story, use paragraphs to develop the sequence of events. Start a new paragraph for each new event, or each time you introduce a change of time or place. At the start of a paragraph, make it clear to the reader how the story has moved on, by showing movement in time or place.

Developing the story in paragraphs

Build each paragraph around an event or important part of the story. For example, here is a paragraph building up to the big event (a football match). The purpose of this paragraph is to contrast the main character's feelings with those of the rest of his class.

*time **adverbials** link the paragraphs showing movement in time*

> In the afternoon everyone became more and more excited as the hour of the match approached. Most of 6B found it hard to concentrate on their history project, particularly when they could hear the preparations going on outside. Max, on the other hand, was quite happy to bury his head in a book and escape into the past for a while.
>
> After school Max followed the crowd to the football pitch at the side of the school …

develops the theme of the paragraph

mentioning 'the match' and 'the football pitch' links the two paragraphs

new paragraph because the story moves on to the next event and setting

Linking paragraphs with adverbials

Use linking adverbials at the start of paragraphs to tell your reader about movements in time. For example:

Suddenly,…   The next day,…   Later,…   After a while,…   Eventually,…

Or use adverbials to keep your reader informed of changes in setting. For example:

Back at school,…   On the other side of the river,…   Outside,…   In the cellar,…

Changing the focus

Start a new paragraph if there is a change in focus – for example, focusing on a different character. In the first sentence, make the links between the paragraphs clear to your reader. For example:

Jack was not the only one with a problem. Megan…

the focus moves onto Megan and a new problem is about to be revealed

these words refer back to the paragraph before, connecting the two paragraphs

Test yourself

Here is the end of a paragraph from a story. Write a suitable opening sentence for the next paragraph.

Mrs Donaldson rambled on, telling us her strange stories. She seemed desperate to show us some old photographs and insisted we go into the loft to find them as soon as we finished our tea.

Remember

Use a series of clearly linked paragraphs to develop the plot, setting and characters in your story.

Composing sentences

As you write each paragraph of your story, develop the plot with detail and description. Picture the events, characters and setting so you can describe them clearly for your reader.

Write the story sentence by sentence. Choose words carefully and think about how you structure your sentences. Keep rereading as you write, to check that all the sentences work together.

Composing sentences

Say a sentence in your head and think about whether you could improve it before writing it down. For example:

> He walked through the wood.

Think about how you could add more detail to create a particular effect. You could use **noun phrases**, **adverbials** or a **subordinate clause**. Look at the two very different effects below.

Terrified, he scrambled through the grasping branches of the trees. ← creates a feeling of *fear*

Whistling quietly, he sauntered through the welcome shade of the woods. ← sounds relaxed and *pleasant*

Choosing sentence structures

Writing usually sounds best if you vary your sentences, using different openings and structures to develop the ideas. Reread each paragraph to check the effect of your sentence structures. For example, look at the different ways subordinate clauses have been used here.

> The door, which was slowly closing, was their only chance of escape. They wildly ran through the trees, staggering and half falling towards the entrance. Diving forward, they scrambled through the gap just as the door slammed shut. They lay in a breathless heap – safe!

You could use:

- short sentences for pace, drama or impact

> He ran.   All was silent.

- an exclamation to surprise or grab the reader's attention
- questions to draw the reader in and make them think about what might happen next

> Surely it would not matter if she took just one bite? What could happen?

- sentence fragments, unfinished sentences or an ellipsis (…) at the end of a paragraph.

Test yourself

Write two or three carefully chosen sentences to describe these events in a more interesting way.

Rosie went in the cave. She looked for the treasure chest.

Remember

Rehearse and improve sentences before you write them. Keep rereading to check the effect, and make changes where you need to.

Creating an effect

Good stories are full of powerful, exciting words and imaginative use of language and sentence structure.

As a story writer, you should always choose the best word, rather than the first word that comes into your head. Choose the word that describes exactly or creates the effect you want. Use a **thesaurus** to help you replace words and expressions you use every day.

When **editing**, think about whether the words you have used accurately describe things in your story. Choose expanded noun phrases to create vivid word pictures.

a ~~big shiny~~ *magnificent gleaming sports* car

an ~~old tatty car~~ *antiquated ramshackle motor*

Try to think about the key feature. One **adjective** is usually better than four.

He crept along the ~~narrow, thin, dark, scary~~ *unlit* path.

Remember the effect you want to achieve, and make sure you choose words that will help. **Synonyms** can have different shades of meaning and so might create different effects.

Hurriedly, we ~~scampered scuttled~~ *scrambled* up the hill. ⟵ sounds more panicked

~~A strange fog~~ An *eerie mist* descended. ⟵ sounds more mysterious

Sometimes you might choose words to make your writing sound more story-like or to entertain the reader. You might think about the sound of words as well as their meaning.

the dank, dingy dungeon ⟵ **alliteration**

BOING! ⟵ **onomatopoeia**

The dishevelled urchin begged for meagre crusts. ⟵ *story language*

Grammar and language

You can use grammar and language to keep your story interesting. You can do this at different stages in your story. Use suspense to draw your readers in, delay the action and keep them guessing. Try suggesting hidden dangers and creating doubt – then you can surprise your reader with quick action-packed events. You could use:

- **noun phrases** for sensory description to build atmosphere
- **pronouns** such as 'someone' or 'something' to help create a sense of mystery
- **passive verbs** to keep the 'doer' hidden: The window had been smashed.
- **adverbials** that create surprise: suddenly   without warning   from nowhere
- **modal verbs** or **adverbs** to suggest possibilities: It could still be there.   Maybe it was waiting inside.
- **similes**, **metaphors** and **personification** to create mood: An angry sky glowered overhead.
- **alliteration** and **onomatopoeia** to suggest intriguing or worrying sounds: drip, drip, drip

Test yourself

Imagine that the main character in a story is faced with a choice – to press the red button or the blue button. Only the right choice will get them back home safely. Write this part of the story using grammar and vocabulary to build tension and excitement.

Remember

Choose words that create clear pictures and engage the reader. Use grammar and language to help make your story effective.

Developing characters

Stories need interesting characters. The main characters in your story need to be more than just names.

Picture your characters in your head. Decide what sort of person a character is so you can think about how he or she would behave, speak or feel at different points in the story. Feed these details in as you write.

Think about stories you have read and how authors show rather than tell you about characters, through carefully chosen details, description, dialogue and actions. There are lots of ways you can do this.

Descriptive detail

Include a few key details to describe the character's appearance. Choose features that help your reader picture the character but also show their personality.

> Emma had a thin face and dark, thoughtful eyes.

Actions and dialogue

A character's actions and dialogue should show what sort of person the character is. For example, here a character's shyness is shown through his actions.

> Luke lingered at the back of the crowd of jostling bodies, hoping to remain hidden from view.

Showing feelings

Show the feelings of the main character(s) and their reaction to events. Use details, powerful **verbs** and **adverbs** that show rather than tell the reader. For example:

> Hamza stood anxiously on the touchline, his whole body trembling.

Showing thoughts and intentions

Show the thoughts of different characters in the story through their actions and reactions as well as through comments. For example:

> The crowd groaned. He sank to the ground in despair. He thought it was over.

Contrasting characters

Contrasting characters can work well in a story. You can show the differences between them in their different reactions to events. For example:

> While Charlie hid from view, Zain enjoyed being the centre of attention.

Test yourself

Write two sentences to show this character, one using descriptive details, one using actions.

Jess – slightly bossy, very organised

Remember

Show character through actions, dialogue and carefully chosen details.

Settings and atmosphere

You should have a clear picture in your head of when and where your story takes place. You can then create a picture of this setting for your reader. Think about stories you have read and how the authors create the settings using description and various small details about sights and sounds.

Remember that authors also use description of a setting to help create mood and atmosphere. You can create a feeling about a place and what might happen there.

Familiar settings

If the setting is a familiar one, you don't need to describe every detail. The reader will be able to picture it from a few key details. Choose sights or sounds that capture the scene and mood for the reader.

> The classroom was flooded with excited chatter and discarded scraps of paper.

Unfamiliar settings

If your story has a historical or fantasy setting, you will need to describe the setting in more detail. Have a clear picture in your head and include a longer description focusing on the more unusual details, so the reader can picture it too.

> The shelves on the walls were stacked with glass containers each holding a different coloured liquid. Some liquids were bubbling, some were fizzing. Some jars were clear, some were murky…

Creating atmosphere

You can also use details about the setting to create mood or atmosphere in your story. Remember that weather and time of day are also part of the setting. These can be useful for developing different moods and atmospheres. Compare these two examples:

> It was late and the sky was growing dark. Strange scuttling noises came from among the overhanging trees.

different types of light and sounds are particularly useful for creating mood and atmosphere

> Laughter echoed in the lazy afternoon sunshine.

Test yourself

In an adventure story the main character is looking for someone in a busy supermarket. Note some details about the setting to use in this part of the story.

Remember

Describe key details about the setting. Choose details that also help to create mood or atmosphere.

Using dialogue

Dialogue is an important part of a story. However, make sure that the dialogue you write is always useful to the plot or character development, not just a pointless conversation. Don't use too much dialogue – it can slow your story down. Try to keep a balance between action, dialogue and description.

Use dialogue between characters to introduce new information about events or to reveal something about the characters. A conversation between two characters might show their feelings or reactions to events, or illustrate the relationship between them.

Direct speech

Use **direct speech** at key moments in your story to introduce an important event or to show something about the characters.

> 'Hi there,' shouted Jamie, from among a crowd of people.
> 'Oh, hello Jamie,' said Ali shyly.
> 'Great day for a football match, don't you think?'
> 'I suppose it is. I'd forgotten it was the match tonight,' admitted Ali.

This dialogue introduces an important event (the football match). It also shows something about the characters (Ali is shy and much less interested in the match than Jamie).

Interesting speech verbs

When writing direct speech, don't keep using 'said'. Choose other speech **verbs** that either tell the reader something about the characters or suggest their feelings.

screamed	moaned	muttered	murmured
suggested	shrieked	chuckled	snapped

Or use **adverbs** that describe how a character says something – another way to suggest their feelings.

coldly	miserably	bravely	awkwardly
nervously	thoughtfully	cautiously	sarcastically

Reported speech

As well as mixing direct speech with description and action for variety, you can also use reported speech to summarise quickly what was said. For example:

> Ali admitted that he had forgotten about the match.

Test yourself

In a story, one of the characters finds an old key. Write a short dialogue between two characters to introduce this important new event.

Remember

Use dialogue to introduce a new event in the story or to show what characters are like.

Writing a play script

Sometimes stories are presented as scripts to be performed. A script uses dialogue and action to tell the story rather than narrative and description. When reading or performing a script, use your voice to show the characters and do the actions necessary to make the events clear to your audience.

If you are writing a script, think about plays you have read or seen performed. This will help you to develop ideas for writing and presenting your own script.

Planning a script

A play script usually has a series of scenes, set at different times or in different settings. The dialogue within each scene makes it clear what is happening in that part of the story. You can add stage directions to show the actions of characters if they are needed.

> Katherine: What are you doing, Luke?
> Luke: [on his hands and knees] Looking for clues.
>   Someone was here last night – I know it.

When you are writing a script, keep reading it back. Make sure that what is happening in the story is clear to the actors and the audience.

Developing characters

Show the characters, and the relationships between them, through the dialogue. Give each character its own individual style of speech. Try saying lines of dialogue before you write them so you can 'hear' the character and choose the right words.

Adverbs used as stage directions show how lines should be spoken. This can show character or feelings.

> Katherine: [crossly] Luke, stop asking so many questions. You're just so annoying.

Presenting a script

When you are writing a script, think about how they are usually set out. This will help you to present your script so it is easy for the reader to follow.

> Scene 1: An office
>
> *enter Katherine and Luke*
>
> Luke: What a mess! There's paper everywhere.

Test yourself

In this scene, Luke and Katherine are looking for a note. Write how the scene might continue.

Katherine: [anxiously] Hurry up, Luke. Someone might see us.

Remember

Use plays and scripts you have read as models to help you write and present your own script.

Writing for different purposes

Before you begin a piece of non-fiction writing, you need to think about the task and be clear about three things.

- The purpose – why am I writing this?
- The audience – who am I writing it for?
- The form – what am I writing?

This is important because it will help you make decisions about what to write, how to write it and how to organise and present your writing.

Make sure you know exactly what is required before you start planning or writing, so you can think about the different features used in that form of writing.

Different purposes, different audiences

There are many different purposes or reasons for writing. You might need to:

- recount, describe or instruct
- explain, inform or persuade
- discuss, compare or recommend.

Your audience might be anyone, from the general public to children in another school.

Different forms

You might be asked, or choose, to produce various different forms of writing, including:

- an interview, news report or magazine article
- a letter, journal or diary.

Here is an example of a writing task. The purpose, audience and form have been highlighted. Think about what this information tells you about the piece of writing required.

form: a letter – these need to be set out in a particular way

> Your class wants to set up a small vegetable garden in the school grounds. Write a letter to the school's board of governors to explain your ideas and persuade them to give you a small amount of money to buy materials.

*audience: an official group – the letter will need to sound **formal***

purpose: to explain and persuade – it will need reasons why it is a good idea

Model texts

Once you know the purpose and form of your writing, think of similar examples you have read. Use these as models to help you decide what to write, how it should sound and how you could organise and present it.

Test yourself

Here is a writing task. Identify the purpose and audience. Choose a suitable form for the piece of writing.

A school is making some changes to school dinners. It wants to explain the changes to parents.

Remember

Be clear about the purpose, audience and form for your writing. Think of similar texts you have read.

Planning: gathering ideas

Whatever you are writing, first you need some ideas. Don't just start writing ideas in the order they come into your head – it is important to plan your writing first.

The first stage in planning is gathering your ideas and deciding what to include. Think about the purpose, audience and form of the writing as you select your content. Choose **facts**, ideas and details that will inform and interest the reader, as well as achieving your purpose.

Noting and developing ideas

Note your ideas, using words or brief **phrases**. Begin to put related points or similar ideas together.

You might sometimes use a spider diagram like this to help you gather and sort your ideas. This example shows facts gathered about penguins for an entry in a zoo guidebook. Related facts or pieces of information are put together.

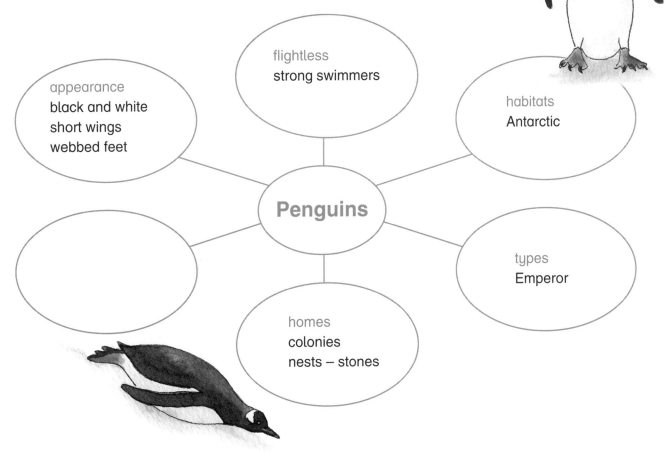

Checking your content

You will need a number of ideas to make your writing convincing. Make sure you have enough detail to develop the ideas as you write. You can use ideas from reading, your own experience and things learnt in other school subjects. If you are writing in an imaginary situation you can invent information, but if you are writing for a real purpose you might need to do further research on the topic.

Planning: organising ideas

Non-fiction writing must be organised. It should have a clear shape, with an introduction, middle section (the main part) and conclusion. It should also be easy to follow, with the ideas or points linking together in a logical order. So once you have your ideas, the next stage is to put them in order and plan the stages in your writing: the beginning, the main sequence of ideas and the ending.

Choosing a planning frame

A planning frame or template will help you plan your piece of writing. But different types of non-fiction text are organised in different ways, so you need to choose a planning frame that will help you shape or **structure** that particular text. For example, if you are:

- recounting a series of events, you could use a timeline
- explaining a sequence of steps or stages in a process, you could use a flowchart
- comparing two things, ideas or different points of view, you could use columns headed 'same and different' or 'for and against'
- describing or giving information on different aspects of a topic, you could use a spider diagram like the one on page 79.

Using your planning frame

Here is an example of a planning frame used to plan an information leaflet about a city farm. The writer has used it to plan the main sections of the leaflet and to note a few details or examples to include in each section.

Introduction
- welcome, explain purpose

History
- set up 3 yrs ago, volunteers, latest arrivals – bees

Future plans
- extend stables, café, children's playground

Things to see and do
- farm tour, feed animals, pets corner, farm shop

Important information & reminders
- feeding animals, gates

Conclusion
- thank you, visit again

← *good planning frame for a leaflet – it shows what will be in each section of it*

← *ideas in note form – single words, brief **phrases***

← *logical order – history of farm, followed by future plans*

Remember
Choose a suitable planning frame or template to help you organise and order your ideas.

Test yourself
You have been asked to write an article for your local newspaper on leisure activities available for young people in your local area. Use a planning frame like this one to make a plan for the article.

Formal or informal

Before you start writing, it is important to think about who you are writing for – your audience. This will help you decide whether your writing should be **formal** or **informal**.

Informal writing is generally used if you are writing for someone you know personally or for a younger audience, or if you want to seem friendly. Formal writing is used when you are writing for someone you do not know or when you want to be taken seriously.

As you write, it is important to keep your reader in mind so that you use the right sort of language and grammar.

Informal writing

Informal writing sounds more like ordinary speech. It is chatty and uses everyday language. If you are writing in an informal style, imagine you are speaking to a friend. Make it sound like a normal conversation.

Here is an extract from a letter written to a friend. Look at the language and grammar features showing that it is an informal letter.

exclamations

What an experience! I am never going on holiday with my family again – NEVER! First the car broke down. We'd only just made it onto the motorway. Great, isn't it?

shortened forms

questions with **question tags**

Formal writing

In contrast, formal writing sounds very different to normal speech. If you are writing in a formal style, imagine yourself as an adult or an important and knowledgeable person. Think about how this person would say or write things.

Here is an extract from a formal letter. Look at the language and grammar features showing its formal style.

polite formal **phrases**

It has come to our notice that this area is adjacent to a planned housing development and that Redbridge Wood may be under threat. If Redbridge Wood were to be destroyed, it would be a disaster for wildlife.

The wood is often visited by...

formal, technical words

the **subjunctive verb** *form (only found in formal speech and writing) – using 'were' rather than 'was' (for example, 'If I were...', 'If he were...')*

passive

Test yourself

Rewrite this sentence so that it sounds more formal.

If the money was available, we'd do up the play area.

Remember

Choose words and grammar that will help to make your writing sound suitably formal or informal.

Writer's voice

Make your writing sound convincing. To do this you need to choose the right 'voice' for your purpose, audience and form. Think about texts you have read and how they sounded. Get the sound of the writer's voice in your head. Then copy that voice in your writing. Say sentences in your head before you write them down and keep reading back to check that you have kept the right tone and voice all through.

Different voices

There are many examples of writers' voices you might use, depending on the audience, form and purpose of your writing, including:

- the knowledgeable expert, who states things clearly and sounds confident and informed about the subject

- the hidden persuader, who uses language to sound convincing and believable:

> Of course...   Obviously...   Clearly...
> Everyone wants...   It is only fair...   No wonder...

- the commanding instructor, who confidently tells the reader what to do:

  Divide the players into two teams of five.

- the concise news reporter, who tells the reader all the details:

  Mrs Willows, aged 76, was visiting her daughter when the accident happened.

- the friendly voice of personal writing, as used in a diary or a letter to a friend, or to appeal directly to the audience.

Impersonal voice

Formal writing often needs an impersonal voice. Use grammatical features to make your writing sound more impersonal. For example, rather than writing 'I think', try:

> Some people say...   Many people believe...   It is known that...

I think mobile phones should be banned in school.   ← *sounds personal*

Some people believe that mobile phones should be banned in school.   ← *impersonal*

Or try using **passive verb** forms, which hide the 'doer' of the action.

We use a microscope to see the cells.   ← *personal*

A microscope is used to see the cells.   ← *impersonal*

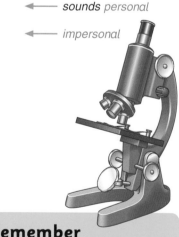

Test yourself

Rewrite these sentences using the passive to make them sound impersonal.
1. We wrote a letter to the head teacher.
2. We use a lot of paper every day.

Remember

Choose an appropriate writer's voice and keep this voice in mind as you write.

Introductions

Always start with an introduction – a sentence or short paragraph that introduces the topic and makes clear the purpose of the writing.

A good introduction should also capture the interest of the reader.

Setting the scene

Often the introduction will need to provide some context or background information for the reader. It might need to set the scene, explain an issue or make clear the purpose of the writing.

For example, here is an introduction for a leaflet discussing the pros and cons of building a ring road. It provides the reader with background information and explains the purpose of the leaflet.

> It has been suggested that a ring road should be built around the town of Midvale. This would ease the traffic congestion within the town centre. However, there are people opposed to such a development. This leaflet aims to summarise the main points on each side of the argument.

Fitting the purpose, form and audience

The length and style of the introduction should fit the purpose, form and audience of the writing. For example, here is an introductory sentence for a set of instructions to appear in a children's comic.

sounds appealing and fun – aimed at young audience

> Halloween is nearly here, so why not follow these instructions and carve a seriously spooky pumpkin.

makes the purpose clear – instructions for how to make something

Here are some other examples of introductions for different forms of writing.

- News reports usually begin with a headline and an opening sentence that summarises what the story is about:

> **City centre in gridlock**
>
> The city centre was closed for two hours yesterday morning when an accident caused traffic chaos in Manchester.

- Factual information often begins by defining the topic:

> Penguins are large flightless birds.

> Manchester United is one of the most successful Premiership teams.

- Accounts might begin by setting the scene (who, what, where, when, why):

> On the 3 August 1492 Christopher Columbus set sail from Spain on a voyage of discovery.

Test yourself

Write an introduction for a magazine article, with the title 'Are footballers paid too much money?'

Remember

The introduction should set up the piece of writing and provide background information for the reader.

Conclusions

Always bring your writing to a clear ending or conclusion. This might be summing up, restating the main point(s) or adding a final comment. A conclusion helps to bring the writing to a tidy end, rather than sounding as if you have simply run out of ideas.

Before writing a conclusion, reread what you have already written. Then try rehearsing your conclusion in your head before you write it.

Ways of concluding

Closing a piece of non-fiction writing can be difficult. You could:

- give an overall comment on the event or activity described

> Despite all the problems, it was probably the best holiday we've ever had.

- summarise or restate a point made at the start

> There are valuable arguments both for and against building the new ring road. It is important that all points of view are considered when reaching a decision on this important local issue.

- relate the information to the reader

> Like people all over the world, you will experience these changes in weather patterns caused by global warming.

- give an **opinion** or evaluation, if appropriate.

> Overall,…   After great consideration,…   All in all,…

Fitting the purpose, form and audience

Choose a conclusion that fits the purpose, audience and form of your writing. Here are some other examples of conclusions for different forms of writing.

- Instructions might end with a final statement telling the reader that the process is now complete:

> Now you can sit back and enjoy your crunchy cookies.

- A news report might end by bringing events up to date or by referring to events in the future:

> United's next match is against City on Wednesday night.

- A persuasive leaflet or advert might end with a short, snappy slogan:

> Don't throw it away – recycle today!
>
>

Test yourself

Write a conclusion for the article on different uses of computers that you planned on page 79. Remember that your audience is elderly users.

Remember

Bring your writing to a clear conclusion. Don't just stop when you run out of ideas.

Organising paragraphs

Use paragraphs to help organise your writing. Each paragraph should have a main idea, topic or theme.

Start a new paragraph each time you change topic or introduce a new point. Your plan will help you to write in paragraphs. Each idea or group of ideas noted on your plan will be one paragraph in your writing.

Here is an example of using paragraphs in a letter of complaint.

On arriving at the playground we found that many of the rides were broken and in a dangerous state. One of the see-saws, for example, had been snapped off, leaving a dangerous, rough edge that could have injured one of the children.

this paragraph develops the idea of things being broken

Moreover, the state of the playground itself was disgusting. There was litter everywhere…

new paragraph – it moves onto the subject of litter

links the two paragraphs – signals a new point being made

Linking adverbials

You can use linking **adverbials** at the start of paragraphs to show how the ideas in different paragraphs link together.

For example, if you are adding another point, use these adverbials:

Furthermore,…	Moreover,…	In addition,…
Also,…	What is more,…	Additionally,…

If you are introducing a different or contrasting view, try these adverbials:

However,…	On the other hand,…	In contrast,…	Despite this,…

Other linking devices

You can also use the wording of the first sentence of a new paragraph to link back to the one before, perhaps repeating a word or **phrase**.

Of course, introducing these changes will not be easy.

these words link back to the topic of the previous paragraph

This sentence also introduces the topic of the new paragraph: why it will not be easy.

Test yourself

Complete the second paragraph of the letter of complaint shown above. Then write the first sentence of a new paragraph praising a particularly helpful member of staff.

Remember

Start a new paragraph for each new idea. Use linking devices to show how the paragraphs link together.

Developing paragraphs

Each paragraph should develop an idea or theme. It is a good idea to start a paragraph with a topic sentence – this is a sentence that introduces the main point of the paragraph.

Then in the rest of the paragraph you can expand on that point by explaining it, giving more detail or providing examples to back it up. You can use **adverbials** to help link these ideas together.

Introducing a paragraph

Here is an example of a paragraph that begins with a topic sentence and then explains the point, giving more detail. The paragraph is taken from an e-mail to a company that makes mobile phones. The e-mail outlines a number of problems.

adverbial - it links ideas together

> Firstly, the charger provided with the phone does not seem to be working. When I plug it in, it begins to charge and then switches off. As a result, I have not been able to charge my phone properly for a week. It has now run down completely so I am unable to use it at all.

the topic sentence – it tells you what this paragraph is about

these sentences explain the problem in detail

the paragraph ends by showing the result of the charger not working

Linking ideas within a paragraph

Order your ideas within a paragraph so that they clearly follow on. Show your reader how these ideas link together. Use **conjunctions** and adverbials.

As a result,...	Therefore,...	Consequently,...	so...	← *to show a* result
For example,...	For instance,...	such as...		← *to introduce an example*
However,...	In contrast,...	On the other hand,...	although... but...	← *to contrast ideas*

Reference chains

Within a paragraph, you will usually refer to the same topic a number of times. Rather than repeating the same word or **phrase**, use **pronouns** or alternative **nouns** and noun phrases.

> Penguins cannot fly but they are excellent swimmers. These amazing birds...

Test yourself

Complete the second sentence in this paragraph.

Next week is 'Walk to school week'. Therefore...

Remember

Start each paragraph with a topic sentence. Then develop the point, linking your ideas together.

Composing sentences

Develop your ideas sentence by sentence. Say sentences aloud in your head before writing them down. Construct sentences that clearly express your ideas, points or **facts** and sound right for the type of text you are writing. Use **subordinate clauses** to link, expand and develop ideas. Use adverbials, **prepositions** and noun phrases to add important detail. Keep rereading your writing to see if the sentences work together.

Using adverbials

Use **adverbs** and prepositional phrases to give more detail about how, where or when.
For example, in instructions, adverbials can help explain exactly how to do something:

With the masking tape, carefully cover the edges of the box.

Using noun phrases

Use noun phrases to give clear, precise information without using too many words:

Penguins are flightless birds with short, powerful wings and webbed feet that aid swimming.

Using clauses and conjunctions

Use conjunctions to add subordinate clauses that develop and link ideas together:

While many penguins build nests, the Emperor penguin places its egg on top of its feet.

Use **relative clauses** to add concise extra detail about the **subject**.

Samantha Jones, who works at the school, was first to notice something was wrong.

Don't expand every sentence. A short sentence can be clearer and more powerful.

This is wonderful.

Sentence types for effect

Choose different types of sentence to achieve different effects. You could use:
- questions to attract attention or to make your reader think about the topic:

Have you ever seen... a duck-billed platypus?
Did you know that...?   Can we really let this happen?

- **commands** to appeal or speak directly to your reader:

Start today – set up a recycling box in your classroom.

- short sentences to make an impact:

Disease can kill.

- lists or repeated patterns to enhance the effect:

There were thousands injured, hundreds homeless, too few doctors.

- **semi-colons** to directly contrast two pieces of information:

Polar bears live in the Arctic; penguins live in Antarctica.

Creating an effect

When you are drafting or **editing** a piece of non-fiction writing, think carefully about the grammar and vocabulary choices you make. Try to make your writing interesting and appealing to the reader. Think about your audience, form and purpose. Choose words that help to express **facts** or ideas clearly and precisely.

Words

Think about the purpose, form and audience, as well as the effect you want to achieve. For example, if you are writing an advert you might choose superlatives to exaggerate, or words that will appeal to your reader.

> the coolest colours   the latest designs   exceptional performance

If it is a **formal** piece of writing, use formal words and **phrases** rather than everyday expressions.

> tell you about → inform you of   let → allow   ask → enquire

Think about the topic. Technical words will usually sound better than everyday words. For example, in a report on recycling, the changes below are more accurate and informative.

> It is then made into ~~mush~~ pulp.   The gases escape into the ~~sky~~ atmosphere.

Sometimes one precise word expresses an idea better than several everyday words.

> ~~You can use it again~~. It is reusable.

Think about the impact of the word. You might need a stronger word to get an idea across. For example, here the writer strengthens the **adjective** to emphasise the danger.

> This journey was ~~dangerous~~ → extremely dangerous… treacherous… hazardous… perilous.

Changing or adding a word can make a slight but important change to the meaning. For example, when discussing possibilities, you might use **adverbs** and **modal verbs** like this:

> In the future, there will probably be more cars on the road. We ~~will~~ might travel by jet pack.

Grammar and language

Keep the reader's interest through both what you say and how you say it. For example, in a news report you might use:

* direct quotations in inverted commas:

    One terrified survivor said, 'Everything was just swept away.'

* vivid language such as powerful **verbs** and adjectives for emotional impact, to make the reader feel or react:

    The survivors arrived, clutching their pitiful belongings.

* adverbs to express views or comment on the events: Unfortunately,…

Language can be used to create effects in non-fiction writing as well as stories. You could use:

* **figurative language** such as a **simile** to present an idea:

    Its ears are shaped like shells.

* **alliteration** to make something memorable:

    Donna's deserts – dreamy, delicious, delightful!

* puns or word play to amuse or capture the reader's interest.

Remember

Choose the right words to express your ideas and make your meaning clear. Choose language and grammar that will help to engage your reader and increase the impact of your writing.

Test yourself

Rewrite this sentence using more precise and formal words.

We have heard that the local council are thinking of doing away with lollipop ladies and having crossings instead. We want them to think again.

Presenting your writing

Think about how to present your writing to the reader. The presentation should make it easier for the reader to read your text. For example, you might:

- use sub-headings to show how the writing is organised or what each paragraph or section is about
- use underline or larger lettering for parts of the text that you want to stand out
- number points to show that they should be read in a particular order.

Presenting a leaflet

Here is an example of how presentation is used to help guide the reader around a text.

main heading →

slogan bold so it stands out →

The City Farm Project

Enjoy a day down on the farm

Welcome to our visitors

Welcome to the City Farm! We hope you enjoy your trip.

A short history of the project

The City Farm opened in 2008 and has gone from strength to strength. We have more animals every year and the vegetable patch is well established.

The farm's future

Having received more funding in 2015, the City Farm is looking to expand, with the help of volunteers and local fundraisers.

Things for you to see

- milking demonstrations
- unusual animal breeds
- tractor rides
- sheep shearing

← sub-headings to say what each paragraph is about

← bullet point list so you can see at a glance what's there

Presenting different forms of writing

Different forms of writing are presented in different ways. For example, you would present a letter very differently from an information leaflet. Newspapers, instructions, adverts, articles in comics and magazines all have their own special layout features. Whatever form of writing you are asked to produce, think about examples you have seen and how they are set out. Then use these features in your own writing.

Handwriting

You should use joined handwriting for most of the writing you do. Joined handwriting helps you write down ideas quickly and fluently. Keep unjoined letters for headings, sub-headings or the labels on a diagram.

Checking and practising

The most important thing is that your handwriting is clear and readable. Take particular care when writing a final version to be read by others. Watch the size, spacing and slant of your writing so that the finished piece looks neat.

Try to improve the fluency and neatness of your writing. Practise until you can write down what you want to say quickly and clearly. Below are some suggestions for what to check.

Shape – letters and joins

Make sure that all your letters are correctly formed and joined with the correct diagonal and horizontal strokes. Some pairs of letters are best left unjoined – for example, joining from g, j, y, z, x can be messy. Use these as break letters.

g, j, y, z, x

Spacing

Make sure that you use equal spacing, both between the letters within a word and between different words. You should also leave enough space between lines of writing so that the ascenders and descenders of letters do not overlap.

apple beautiful

Straight or slanting

Make sure that the downstrokes of your letters are all parallel (or in line). They should either go straight up and down or all lean slightly at the same angle. Watch particularly your ascenders and descenders – don't let some lean if others are straight. If your writing does slant, it must stay the same throughout the piece of writing.

Special lettering

Sometimes you might use a special style of lettering for effect. For example, on a poster you might use capitals or decorative lettering.

Test yourself

Practise your handwriting by writing a short paragraph of information about yourself. Follow the advice on this page to help you judge your handwriting. Look for any problem areas you need to practise.

Remember

Practise your handwriting so it is fluent, swift, readable and neat.

Answers

Page 4
1 interested, engrossed, fascinated
2 cramped, enclosed, shut up
3 sight, scene, show

Page 5
1 make pure
2 dressed too smartly
3 easily predicted
4 respect, praise
5 wrongly informed
6 feel sorry for, feel sympathy for

Page 6
For example: They will go into the cellar and then probably wish they hadn't.

Page 7
Jack climbs a beanstalk. 2
Jack steals a magic hen. 4
Jack exchanges his cow for beans. 1
Jack chops down the beanstalk. 5
Jack discovers a castle. 3
Ask an adult to listen as you retell the story.

Page 8
Any four of these:
● like a pillow
● soft, comfortable and always there when needed
● the children called her Granny Pringle
● gentle words
● cheery smile
● delicious biscuits

Page 9
He is trying to put off this moment (e.g. 'he walked as slowly as he could'; he 'came to the gate all too quickly'; he looks around, 'hoping for something to distract him'). He is frightened of going inside (e.g. 'he felt a cold fist clench in his stomach').

Page 10
It makes us think perhaps the sisters were not so bad (e.g. perhaps the usual story is 'lies'), and makes Cinderella seem less likeable (e.g. telling lies, using her prettiness).

Page 11
For example:
Structure – builds up to the moment when the box is opened (seeing it, describing it, picking it up); suggests possibilities, making the reader wonder (e.g. 'Perhaps there was something inside.')
Language – gives details about the box (e.g. half-hidden, simple wooden, surprisingly heavy); sounds special, powerful (e.g. 'draw him towards it')

Page 12
to show that the glimpse of sky was very important to the prisoner – it provided his only source of light, his

only reminder of the outside world, and represented freedom

Page 13
Metaphor: 'the cave was a magnet for them' – shows they were drawn to the cave and could not keep away
Simile: 'they felt like explorers on another planet' – shows how they felt inside the cave, as if it was a new and different world

Page 14
Settings – the future, outer space, another planet or galaxy
Characters – space travellers, scientists, robots, aliens
Events – enemies to defeat, being under threat, facing many dangers
Devices – advanced technology, space travel
Ending – peace restored, enemies defeated

Page 15
Sharing and greed. If the brothers had shared the chapati rather than both wanting it all, they would have had half each and the stranger could not have tricked them.

Page 16
You should have:
● given reasons for your choice, referring to features of the story (e.g. plot, story structure, techniques)
● used examples from different parts of the story
● explained who might like it and why

Page 17
You might have referred to different qualities, behaviour or reactions to events in the story.

Page 18
Verse 2: The tide comes in and the girl disappears.
Verse 3: She is found in the sea, drowned.
Verse 4: Fishermen still hear her ghostly call.

Page 19
Verse 1: The western wind was wild and dank with foam; And all alone went she
Verse 2: crept up along the sand; o'er and o'er; round and round
Verse 3: Above the nets at sea; Among the stakes of Dee
Verse 4: The cruel crawling foam; The cruel hungry foam

Page 20
1 rolling, cruel, crawling, hungry
2 They make us think about the sea being responsible for the girl's death (e.g. 'cruel'; 'hungry' sounds like it swallowed her up; 'crawling' reminds us of how the tide crept in, in verse 2).

Page 21
This simile describes the power and sudden movement of the eagle as it dives down. It also helps to suggest the deadly result of the eagle swooping on its unsuspecting prey.

Page 22
rhythm, rhyme, repeated patterns

Page 23
They spell the word 'frost' which is what the line is describing.

Page 24
● organised in chronological or time order
● describes the history and development of cars
● probably won't explain how they work
● could read it in order or use the headings to find information

Page 25
1 report, information book, encyclopedia
2 recipe, cookbook
3 autobiography

Page 26
1 The inner and outer planets
2 inner – outer
small – huge
rocky and solid – gas and liquid
no/few moons – many moons
nearer to the Sun – further away
shorter orbit time – longer orbit time

Page 27
1 Mercury – closest to the Sun; small and rocky; 88 days; no moons
Jupiter – fifth from the Sun; huge and made of gas; 12 years; many moons
2 Earth has one moon but Mercury has none; or Earth is further away from the Sun and has a longer orbit time

Page 28
1 Yes – they are much bigger/more powerful than humans, and if they are threatened they could charge at you or injure you with their tusks.
2 Yes – in the past humans have hunted elephants for their tusks.

Page 29
Elephants and humans might need to be protected from each other – to stop humans hunting elephants for their tusks, and to stop elephants eating farmers' crops.

Page 30
She is the best current writer of realistic stories.

Page 31
The writer likes spiders and thinks we

should too (e.g. 'captivating creatures', 'deserve our respect', 'should be admired').

Page 32
1 easy to refer to when collecting the items
2 to show the order in which to perform the steps
3 to make clear some of the more difficult steps

Page 33
Two of these:
- to emphasise the huge quantities of meat it eats and that it is always hunting for food
- to make the reader picture the huge, gaping mouth
- to interest or amuse the reader so they think more about the dinosaur's eating habits

Page 34
Use the example on page 34 as a model for your answer, using key phrases and examples from your texts.

Page 35
Possible examples:
1 He could have gone left or right but he went straight on.
2 She opened the door and looked inside but the room was empty.
3 We could hurry and walk there or we could catch the bus.

Page 36
Possible examples (they must have the correct sentence punctuation):
Statement: It is made with real fruit.
Question: Which flavour will you choose?
Command: Taste it today.
Exclamation: How delicious!

Page 37
1 carefully, quietly
2 Carefully, Jade lifted the latch ...

Page 38
Possible examples:
1 The frightened child walked down the busy high street.
2 The exhausted children came to a neat, little cottage with a blue door.
3 The wise old sailor watched the stormy sea.

Page 39
although

Page 40
Sophie, who was desperate to escape, was breathing rapidly.
(You could also miss out 'who was'.)

Page 41
Possible sentences:
1 Although his knees were shaking, he stepped onto the stage.
2 Relieved that they were gone, she climbed down.

Page 42
However,

Page 43
1 The machine was clanking and looked like it was about to explode.
2 It had been like this before. I knew what to do.

Page 44
1 This might solve the problem.
2 They will be here soon. ← most likely
3 It should be warm in summer.
4 I could go to the library.

Page 45
Amy put the hat on. It was too big and fell over her eyes. 'This can't be mine,' thought Amy. 'It must be Ed's.'

Page 46
weren't → wasn't   good → well

Page 47
some = determiner; run = noun; after = preposition

Page 48
Possible synonyms:
- worried – anxious, apprehensive
- terrible – atrocious, dreadful

Page 49
1 disobey
2 imperfect, flawed
3 backwards
4 deflate, let down
5 important
6 fail

Page 50
Many people keep animals as pets. Cats and dogs are particularly popular. Other people prefer smaller animals such as gerbils or hamsters. Which do you prefer?

Page 51
1 Mr Roberts, my teacher, is very strange.
2 First, sieve the flour into the bowl.
3 Although it was very late, we were wide awake.

Page 52
'Where are you?' Kris shouted.
'I'm over here, behind the fireplace. There's some sort of secret tunnel,' said a muffled voice.
'How did you get in there?' asked Kris, feeling around the fireplace for a lever or handle.

Page 53
1 The twins won't go to Amelia's house.
2 The jugglers wouldn't laugh at Coco the clown's tricks.

Page 54
1 Mr Hawkins (the head teacher) wrote to all the parents. (commas or dashes also possible)

Page 55
2 For dinner, it was sprouts – yuk – and shepherd's pie. (brackets also possible)
3 Kevin, smiling broadly, stepped onto the stage. (brackets or dashes also possible)

Page 55
1 The days were hot and dry; the nights were very cold.
2 We had one chance: find the missing key.
3 They divided the books into three piles: fiction, non-fiction and poetry.
4 Some people were amazed; some were horrified.

Page 56
man-eating – to show that it is monsters who eat people rather than a man who is eating monsters

Page 57
Use page 57 to help you find the tricky parts and learn these spellings.

Page 58
1 des/pe/rate
2 rel/e/vant
3 par/lia/ment
4 cat/e/go/ry

Page 59
1 delicious
2 ridiculous
3 nutrition/tious/ent
4 incredible
5 conven/ient/ence
6 interference

Page 60
1 beautiful
2 earlier
3 arrival
4 immature
5 dishearten
6 co-ordinate

Page 61
1 replaceable
2 outrageous
3 definitely
4 probably
5 transferred
6 reference

Page 62
1 island
2 thistle
3 accident
4 excellent
5 answer
6 sacrifice
7 doubt
8 prejudice

Page 63
1 couple
2 system
3 guarantee
4 squirrel
5 nuisance
6 awkward

Page 64

Use pages 57–64 to help you find the tricky parts and learn these spellings.

Page 65

1 allowed – aloud
2 guessed – guest
3 draft – draught
4 led – lead
5 passed – past

Page 66

For example, notes like this:
- Real life characters – brother and sister (Lee, Beth)
- Computer game characters – evil Empress
- Real life setting – Beth's bedroom
- Computer game setting – Planet Zelda, home of evil Empress, lots of robots
- Events – transported to Planet Zelda
- Dangers – captured by evil Empress

Page 67

For example:
- Opening – playing on computer
- Events – transported to Planet Zelda, captured by Empress, escapes using knowledge of the game, returns to bedroom
- Ending – 'won't play that game again'

Page 68

For example: Ethan walking his dog – found UFO in quarry – tried taking photo – captured by aliens – taken on UFO – about to take off – escaped down waste chute – watched UFO leave – but no photo, no proof …

Page 69

For example: And you know what happened then? It started to bucket down!

Page 70

For example:
- Opening – The screen on the computer lit up with the vivid landscape of Planet Zelda.
- Ending – 'I'm all for realistic adventures,' said Beth. 'But that was a little too real!'

Page 71

Here are two examples:
- Up in the loft it was dark and dusty.
- After tea, Mrs Donaldson produced a torch.

Page 72

For example: Crouching low, Rosie scrambled her way into the darkness of the cave. The faint light of her torch cast shadows on the wet walls as she searched the darkest corners looking for the missing treasure chest.

Page 73

For example: Two buttons – one red, one blue. Which one should she choose? One would get them home safely, but if she chose the wrong one … who knows what might happen. Red or blue? What a decision to have to make.

Page 74

For example:
Description: Jess always looked smart – her hair neatly tied back, her clothes clean and tidy, her school bag (with just the right books in) efficiently carried on her shoulder.
Actions: Jess entered the room and strode over to where her friends were sitting – time to get them organised!

Page 75

For example:
- aisles blocked with shoppers and trolleys
- a wall of baked bean tins
- the neon colours of special offer signs
- grumbling queues snaking towards the checkouts

Page 76

Here is an example of a possible dialogue – check that you have punctuated it correctly:
'Hey, look at this key. I found it in that bag of rubbish,' said Tarik.
'It's just an old key,' grumbled Sheena, grabbing an armful of rubbish. 'It's not much use. Throw it away and come and help me clear this.'
'But it must belong to something. Perhaps it's something in that bag,' said Tarik thoughtfully.

Page 77

For example:
Luke: [searching through papers] Just give me a second. It must be somewhere.
Katherine: How did I ever let you talk me into this?
Luke: Come on, you want to know what it says as much as me.
Katherine: Well, I suppose ...
Luke: Aha ....
Katherine: [excitedly] Is that it?

Page 78

Purpose: to explain changes and to persuade them that the changes are a good idea
Audience: parents
Form: leaflet or letter

Page 79

Possible headings (with your own notes):
- letters and writing
- keeping in touch
- finding out information
- shopping
- photography
- games and entertainment

Page 80

For example:
- Introduction – purpose; describe local area
- Sports facilities – playing fields, pool,
- local junior football team; no tennis courts
- Entertainment facilities – dance studio, youth club; no cinema
- Parks, playgrounds – Bankside Park, toddlers playground; no skatepark
- New ideas – young people's interests
- Conclusion – overall comment on current situation and ideas for the future

Page 81

For example: If the money were available, we would renovate the play area.

Page 82

1 A letter was written to the head teacher.
2 A lot of paper is used every day.

Page 83

For example: Premiership footballers receive huge salaries. Some people believe that this is a fair reward for their skills, talent and hard work. Others feel that they do not deserve this much money.

Page 84

For example: As you can see, a computer could be a really useful addition to your home. Why not sign up to a class and give it a try?

Page 85

For example, you could go on to say:
There were paper bags floating in the paddling pool and drink cans lying on the grass. The bins were overflowing. They obviously had not been emptied for some time.
In contrast, I would like to praise the particularly helpful member of staff who runs the refreshments kiosk next to the playground…

Page 86

For example: Therefore we are asking all parents to leave the car at home.

Page 87

For example: Police reported that some drivers continued to speed along the motorway, even though it was extremely foggy.

Page 88

For example: It has come to our attention that the local council are contemplating replacing the traditional school crossing patrol with pelican crossings. We would like them to reconsider.

Page 89

- heading, sub-headings
- numbered points
- diagram to show what to do

Page 90

Use the tips on page 90 to help you judge your handwriting.

Glossary

active	in an active sentence the **subject** performs the action (e.g. Mark paid the fine.) (compare with **passive**)
adjective	a word that describes or adds to a **noun** (e.g. the rough sea)
adverb	a word adds to a **verb** or sentence, giving extra information such as how, where, when (e.g. He paid the fine reluctantly.)
adverbial	a word or **phrase** that works like an **adverb**, adding meaning to a **clause** (e.g. We leave in five days.)
alliteration	a sound effect created when words beginning with the same sound are placed close together (e.g. He was furiously flinging flans.)
ambiguity	when the meaning is not clear – there is more than one possible meaning
antonym	words with the opposite meaning (e.g. hot – cold) (compare with **synonym**)
clause	part of a sentence which contains a **verb** (e.g. the pile of boxes wobbled) – it can form a complete sentence on its own or be part of a longer sentence (compare with **phrase**)
cohesion	when the parts of a text link together
command	a type of sentence that gives an order (e.g. Take the plate back.)
conjunction	a word that links two parts of a sentence (e.g. but, because, when)
consonant letter	all the letters in the alphabet apart from the five **vowel letters** (compare with **vowel letter**)
determiner	a word that goes before a **noun** (e.g. a, the, this, these, my, some)
direct speech	writing down the words spoken by someone, using inverted commas
edit	to check a piece of writing for grammatical errors, and words/**phrases** that could be clearer or more effective, and to make changes to improve it (compare with **proofread**)
fact	something that is generally accepted to be true, with clear evidence to support it (compare with **opinion**)
figurative language	the use of **metaphors** and **similes** to create an effect for the reader
formal	language chosen for a serious purpose, using **Standard English** to make a good impression on the audience (e.g. as in reports, official letters) (compare with **informal**)
homophone	words with the same sound but different meanings and usually different spellings (e.g. bear – bare)
hyphen	a small dash (-) used to join words, to show that they go together (e.g. user-friendly)
infer	to draw out ideas from the information given
informal	language chosen for everyday speech and writing with people you know (compare with **formal**)
metaphor	a type of **figurative language** that describes the subject in terms of something else (e.g. The icicles were spikes of broken glass.) (compare with **simile**)
mnemonic	a trick to help you remember something (e.g. a saying, rhyme, or chant)
modal verb	**verbs** that are used with other verbs to show possibility (e.g. will, could, might, may)
noun	a word that names a thing, person or place (e.g. girl, gentleman, table, pencil)
object	something or someone affected by an action – it comes after a **verb** (e.g. I hit the ball.) (compare with **subject**)
onomatopoeia	words that sound like the noise they are describing (e.g. splash, hiss, splat)
opinion	an idea, belief or point of view held by some people, but one that cannot be proved definitely true (compare with **fact**)
parenthesis	a word, **phrase** or **clause** dropped into the middle of a sentence (e.g. She is, unfortunately, wrong.)

passive	a passive sentence is the opposite of an **active** one, because the **object** of the sentence becomes the **subject** (e.g. The fine was paid [by Mark].) – the original subject of the sentence (Mark) might not be mentioned at all (compare with **active**)
person	when writing in the first person you refer to yourself (I, we); in the second person you refer to the reader (you): in the third person you refer to someone else (he, she, they)
personification	when a writer describes something as if it were human, giving it human feelings, actions or thoughts (e.g. Night crept up on us.)
phrase	a group of words that go together, but with no **verb** (e.g. the pile of boxes – a **noun** phrase) (compare with **clause**)
précis	a written summary of the main ideas in a longer text
predict	to say what is likely to happen or be the result of something
prefix	part of a word – it is added to the beginning of a **root word** to change its meaning (e.g. unpopular) (compare with **suffix**)
preposition	a word that describes where or when (e.g. in, on, by, over) and is usually followed by a **noun** or noun **phrase** to make a **prepositional phrase** (e.g. in two days; along the lane)
pronoun	a word used in place of a **noun** (e.g. I, she, him, it)
proofread	to make final checks on a piece of writing, correcting punctuation and spelling errors (compare with **edit**)
question tag	a brief question added to the end of a statement to make it a question (e.g. isn't it?)
relative clause	a special type of **subordinate clause** that usually starts with a **relative pronoun** and adds information about a **noun** (e.g. the people who live over there)
relative pronoun	a special kind of **pronoun** (e.g. who, which, that)
root word	a base word that can have **prefixes** or **suffixes** added to it to make new words (e.g. 'happy' is the root word of this **word family**: unhappy, happiness, happily)
simile	a type of **figurative language** that compares the subject with something else using the words 'like' or 'as' (e.g. He runs like the wind. She is as fast as a cheetah.) (compare with **metaphor**)
Standard English	the form of English that is generally accepted as 'correct' – it is widely used in writing
structure	the shape or pattern of a story, poem or piece of non-fiction, and how it is put together by the writer
subject	the 'doer' of an action – it usually comes before the **verb** (e.g. I hit the ball.) (compare with **object**)
subjunctive	an unusual **verb** form used only in **formal** speech and writing (e.g. If I were …)
subordinate clause	a **clause** added to a main clause or sentence, often starting with a **conjunction**
suffix	part of a word – it is added to the end of a **root word** to make a new word, usually changing its **word class** (e.g. breathless) (compare with **prefix**)
syllable	beats of a word – longer words can be broken down into syllables (e.g. pow/er/ful)
synonym	words with the same or similar meaning (e.g. answer, reply, respond) (compare with **antonym**)
tense	the form of a **verb** used to refer to different times – in English there is past tense and present tense
thesaurus	a reference book that lists words by meaning, in groups of **synonyms**
verb	a doing or being word (e.g. Adrian shivered. He was cold.); they usually have a past and present **tense**
vowel letter	the letters a, e, i, o, u (compare with **consonant letter**)
word class	a group of words with the same grammatical function (e.g. **nouns**, **verbs**, **adjectives**)
word family	words with the same **root word** and related meanings (e.g. build, builder, rebuild)

Index

accounts **25, 34, 42, 83, 84**
actions **8, 9, 11, 74**
active verbs **44**
adjectives **5, 20, 38, 46, 47, 48, 51, 73, 88**
adverbials **37, 42, 51, 71, 73, 85, 86, 87**
adverbs **37, 47, 51, 73, 74, 76, 77, 87, 88**
advert **25, 36, 84, 88, 89**
alliteration **21, 73, 88**
ambiguity **45, 56**
antonyms **49**
apostrophes **53**
atmosphere **12, 75**

brackets **54**

capital letters **50**
characters **6, 7, 8, 9, 17, 66, 67, 74, 77**
checking grammar **46**
clarifying meaning **51, 56**
clauses **35, 39, 40, 41, 47, 51, 54, 55, 87**
colons **55**
commands **36, 87**
commas **51, 52, 54, 56**
comparisons **17, 27, 34**
conclusions **84**
confusing words **46**
conjunctions **35, 39, 47, 86, 87**
consonants **46, 60, 61, 62**
creating an effect **11, 73, 88**

dashes **54**
description **8, 12, 70, 74**
determiners **38, 46, 47**
dialogue **8, 52, 70, 74, 76, 77**
diary **78, 82**
different viewpoints **10, 31**
direct speech **52, 53, 76**
discussion **42**

editing **46, 48**
embedding **40, 51**
endings **7, 68, 70, 84**
events **7, 68**
evidence **28**
exclamation marks **50, 52**
exclamations **36, 50, 52**
explanations **34, 42, 43**

fable **15**
facts **28, 29, 30, 31, 79**
factual accounts **25, 83**
figurative language **13, 21, 33, 88**
first person **10, 69**
formal writing **34, 55, 81, 82, 88**
full stops **50, 52**
future tense **44**

genres **14**

haiku **23**
handwriting **90**
homophones **65**
hyphens **56, 60**

i before e except after c **63**
ideas **26, 28, 66, 79, 80, 86**
illustrations **24, 34**

imagery **21**
inferring **9, 15, 19, 29**
informal speech **36, 53**
informal writing **69, 81**
information gathering **27**
information texts **25**
instructions **25, 83, 87**
introductions **83**
inverted commas **52, 88**

kenning **23**

language for effect **12, 20, 33, 73**
leaflets **89**
letter strings **57**
limerick **22**
lists **51, 55**
looking for clues **9, 15, 19, 29**

message **15**
metaphors **13, 21, 33, 73**
mnemonics **57, 64, 65**
modal verbs **44, 73, 88**
mood **11, 12, 17, 18, 20, 21, 22, 38, 70, 73, 75**
multi-clause sentences **41**

narrative voice **69**
near homophones **65**
newspaper **25, 30, 89**
noun phrases **12, 35, 38, 73, 87**
nouns **5, 38, 47, 50, 51, 65**

objects **35, 44, 46**
onomatopoeia **21, 73**
openings **7, 70, 83**
opinions **16, 25, 28, 30, 31**
overviews **24**

paragraphs **71, 85, 86**
parenthesis **54**
passive verbs **44, 73, 82**
past tense **43**
perfect tense **43**
personification **21, 73**
persuasive texts **25**
phrases **6, 8, 16, 17, 23, 42, 51, 54, 55, 85**
planning **67, 77, 79, 80**
planning frames **67, 80**
play scripts **77**
plot **68**
plural **53, 61**
précis **7, 26**
predictions **6, 14, 24, 44**
prefixes **5, 49, 60**
prepositional phrases **38**
prepositions **37, 47**
present tense **43**
presentation **23, 27, 32, 77, 89**
progressive tenses **43**
pronouns **40, 45, 46, 53, 73, 86**
proofreading **50, 56**
punctuation for meaning and effect **56**

question marks **36, 50, 52**
questions **6, 36**
quotations **22, 31**

reading a story **6**
reading for meaning **4**

reading non-fiction **24**
reading poems **18, 19**
reasons **16, 29**
reciting and reading aloud **22**
recommending stories **16**
relative clauses **40, 87**
relative pronouns **40**
reported speech **76**
reports **25, 30, 42, 54, 78, 83, 84, 87, 88**
rhyme **22**
rhythm **22**
root words **5, 60, 64**

scanning **27, 29**
script **65, 77**
semi-colons **55, 87**
sentence composition **72, 87**
sentence punctuation **50**
sentence structure **72**
sentence types **36, 87**
sentence writing **35, 50**
settings **67, 75**
silent letters **62, 63**
similes **13, 21, 33, 73**
single-clause sentences **35**
skimming **24**
sound patterns **21**
speech marks **52**
speech verbs **76**
spelling difficult words **57, 62, 63, 64**
spelling longer words **58**
spider diagrams **79**
statements **36**
structure **11, 23, 32, 68, 80**
style of story **69**
subjects **35, 36, 44, 46, 87**
subordinate clauses **39, 40, 41, 51, 87**
suffixes **5, 60, 61**
summarising **7, 26**
suspense **11, 14, 16, 73**
syllables **23, 58, 61**
synonyms **4, 48, 73**

technical words **33, 81, 88**
tenses **43, 44, 46**
tension and suspense **11**
themes for stories **15**
thesaurus **48, 73**
third person **10**
titles **14, 15, 24**
traditional stories **15, 66, 68, 69**
tricky words **57, 62, 63, 64**
types of non-fiction text **25**

unstressed letters **58**

verb forms **43, 44, 46**
verbs **12, 20, 35, 36, 41, 47, 49, 65, 76, 88**
voices **69, 82**
vowels **46, 57, 61, 63**

word classes **46, 47, 60**
word endings **59**
word meanings **4, 5**
words for effect **12, 33, 88**
writer's voice **82**
writing for different purposes **78, 83, 84**